RECIPES TO THE RESCUE

THRILLING KITCHEN ADVENTURES... JUST IN THE NICK OF TIME!

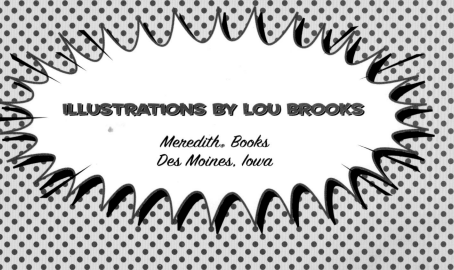

ILLUSTRATIONS BY LOU BROOKS

Meredith® Books
Des Moines, Iowa

MEREDITH® PRESS
AN IMPRINT OF MEREDITH® BOOKS

RECIPES TO THE RESCUE
Editor: Chuck Smothermon
Associate Art Director: Mick Schnepf
Illustrations By Lou Brooks, © 2000
Contributing Writers: Patrick Beach, Ellen Boeke, Winifred Moranville
Contributing Recipe Developers: Ellen Boeke, Karen Brown,
   Amy Cotler, Susan Parenti, Mary Major Williams
Contributing Recipe Editor: Linda Henry
Copy Chief: Catherine Hamrick
Copy and Production Editor: Terri Fredrickson
Contributing Copy Editor: Kim Catanzarite
Contributing Proofreaders: Kathy Eastman, Gretchen Kauffman,
   Debra Morris Smith
Electronic Production Coordinator: Paula Forest
Editorial and Design Assistants: Judy Bailey, Mary Lee Gavin,
   Karen Schirm
Test Kitchen Director: Lynn Blanchard
Test Kitchen Product Supervisor: Lori Wilson
Production Director: Douglas M. Johnston
Book Production Managers: Pam Kvitne, Marjorie J. Schenkelberg

MEREDITH® BOOKS
Editor in Chief: James D. Blume
Design Director: Matt Strelecki
Managing Editor: Gregory H. Kayko

Director, Sales & Marketing, Retail: Michael A. Peterson
Director, Sales & Marketing, Special Markets: Rita McMullen
Director, Sales & Marketing, Home & Garden Center Channel:
   Ray Wolf
Director, Operations: George A. Susral

Vice President, General Manager: Jamie L. Martin

MEREDITH PUBLISHING GROUP
President, Publishing Group: Christopher M. Little
Vice President, Consumer Marketing & Development: Hal Oringer

MEREDITH CORPORATION
Chairman and Chief Executive Officer: William T. Kerr

Chairman of the Executive Committee: E. T. Meredith III

All of us at Meredith® Books are dedicated to providing you with
the information and ideas you need to create delicious foods. We
welcome your comments and suggestions. Write to us at:
Meredith® Books, Cookbook Editorial Department, 1716 Locust
St., Des Moines, IA 50309-3023.

If you would like to purchase any of our books, check wherever
quality books are sold. Visit our website at bhg.com or
bhgbooks.com.

This seal assures you that every
recipe in **RECIPES TO THE RESCUE**
has been tested in the Better
Homes and Gardens® Test
Kitchen. This means that each
recipe is practical and reliable,
and meets high standards of
taste appeal. We guarantee your
satisfaction with this book for as
long as you own it.

CONTENTS

HELP IS ON THE WAY!

YOU MAY ALREADY HAVE A HANDFUL OF GO-TO RECIPES YOU GRAB WHEN YOU'RE UP AGAINST THE CLOCK. BUT HOW MANY TIMES CAN YOU SERVE THE SAME OLD THING BEFORE SOMEONE FINALLY CRIES "UNCLE"?

WELL, MAYBE IT'S TIME FOR SOME NEW OLD FAVORITES—RECIPES YOU KNOW YOU CAN RELY ON WHEN THE CLOCK IS TICKING AND YOU WANT SOMETHING MUCH MORE SATISFYING THAN TAKEOUT. OR WHEN YOU WANT TO ENTERTAIN—BUT NOT AGE 10 YEARS IN THE PROCESS.

RECIPES TO THE RESCUE IS HERE TO HELP. EACH RECIPE WAS CHOSEN WITH THESE STRINGENT GUIDELINES: FIRST, IT HAD TO TASTE GREAT. NEXT, IT COULD TAKE NO MORE THAN 30 MINUTES TO PREPARE AND REQUIRE NO MORE THAN 7 INGREDIENTS. AND, THE INGREDIENTS CALLED FOR HAD TO BE READILY AVAILABLE—NO SENDING ANYONE ON A WILD GOOSE CHASE FOR HARD-TO-FIND FOODS LIKE GALANGA ROOT!

SO, WHAT'S WITH THIS PANTRY BUSINESS? YOU'LL NOTICE THAT AN ENTIRE CHAPTER IS DEVOTED TO MAINTAINING A PANTRY. THE CONCEPT IS SIMPLE: WE ALL KNOW THAT THE THOUGHT OF A TRIP TO THE STORE EXPONENTIALLY DECREASES ONE'S DESIRE TO COOK. SO, BY CALLING ON A WELL-STOCKED PANTRY—AND THIS BOOK OF RECIPES THAT ARE MOSTLY BUILT AROUND THAT PANTRY—YOU'LL NEED LESS TIME FOR PLANNING AND SCHLEPPING. THAT'S HOW

RECIPES TO THE RESCUE GETS YOU HOT ON THE TRAIL OF A GREAT HOME-COOKED MEAL—A.S.A.P.

PANTRY PERILS

THE STORY YOU ARE ABOUT TO READ IS TRUE... A FRIEND CALLS OUT OF THE BLUE. SHE'S IN TOWN FOR THE AFTERNOON AND WOULD LOVE TO SEE YOU. **"COME FOR DINNER,"** YOU SAY CHEERFULLY, WHILE YOU'RE REALLY THINKING, **"WHAT CAN I SERVE?** THERE'S ONLY LEFTOVER TAKE OUT AND A BAG OF BAGELS IN THE REFRIGERATOR!"

THIS DOESN'T HAVE TO BE YOUR STORY. WITH RECIPES TO THE RESCUE AND A LITTLE EXTRA TIME WRITING OUT THAT SHOPPING LIST, YOU'LL ALWAYS BE READY TO COOK AT THE DROP OF A HAT. THE SECRET LIES...BEHIND THE PANTRY DOOR!

WHAT IS A PANTRY?

FORGET ALL ABOUT GRANDMA'S CLOSET FULL OF DUSTY, MOLDERING JARS AND CANNED GOODS. THE PANTRY ISN'T REALLY A PLACE AS MUCH AS IT IS A STATE OF MIND. IT'S A WAY OF THINKING AND PLANNING AHEAD WHEN YOU SHOP SO YOU ALWAYS HAVE BASIC FOOD ITEMS ON HAND.

AFTER YOU'VE STOCKED YOUR PANTRY, TRIPS TO THE SUPERMARKET MAY BE LESS FREQUENT. YOU'LL ONLY NEED TO SHOP FOR PERISHABLE FOODS AND DEPLETED PANTRY ITEMS.

THE PHYSICAL PANTRY IN YOUR HOME IS ANY COOL, DRY PLACE YOU CAN STORE FOOD ITEMS FOR A LENGTH OF TIME, INCLUDING KITCHEN CUPBOARDS, SHELVES—EVEN A LITTLE FLOOR SPACE IN A CLOSET WILL WORK. YOUR REFRIGERATOR AND FREEZER ARE PART OF THE PANTRY, TOO!

HOW DOES IT WORK?

PANTRY ITEMS ARE CONSIDERED DRY GOODS OR STAPLES, THINGS YOU ALWAYS HAVE ON HAND. IDEALLY, THEY WILL KEEP FOR A LONG TIME IN STORAGE, OR ARE FRESH, PERISHABLE FOODS REGULARLY USED UP BEFORE THEY SPOIL. THE RECIPES IN **RECIPES TO THE RESCUE** USE MANY PANTRY ITEMS. THE IDEA IS TO SUBVERT THE NEED TO GO GROCERY SHOPPING EVERY TIME YOU COOK—A MAJOR HURDLE WHEN GETTING FOOD ON THE TABLE. **RECIPES TO THE RESCUE** HELPS YOU AVOID THOSE EXTRA TRIPS TO THE STORE!

THE LISTS ON PAGE 11 ARE TAILORED TO THE RECIPES IN THIS BOOK. YOU MIGHT NOT CONSIDER A FEW OF THESE ITEMS BASIC. BUT IF YOU LOVE THE CHUTNEY-GLAZED RIBEYES, MANGO CHUTNEY WILL BECOME A PANTRY STAPLE.

YOU DON'T HAVE TO BUY EVERYTHING AT ONCE; JUST BUY WHAT YOU THINK YOU'LL EAT FAIRLY OFTEN, AND BUY IN SMALL QUANTITIES SO FOODS STAY FRESH. **BUILD UP YOUR PANTRY GRADUALLY.** TRY A FEW RECIPES AND IF YOU LIKE THEM, STOCK UP ON THE PANTRY FOODS IN THOSE RECIPES.

OF COURSE, NOT ALL INGREDIENTS WORK AS PANTRY STAPLES—FRESH FRUITS, VEGETABLES, MEATS, AND OTHER FOODS ARE PERISHABLE. **THAT'S WHY EACH RECIPE INCLUDES A SEPARATE SHOPPING LIST** MADE UP OF THE FRESH ITEMS YOU'LL NEED TO COMPLETE THE RECIPE, OVER AND ABOVE THE STOCKED PANTRY ITEMS. **RECIPES THAT CAN BE PREPARED ENTIRELY FROM PANTRY ITEMS HAVE BEEN FLAGGED.**

REFRIGERATED AND FROZEN ITEMS

THESE FOODS GENERALLY HAVE A SHORT SHELF LIFE. BUY ONLY THOSE THAT YOU CONSUME WITH FREQUENCY, SUCH AS MILK OR EGGS. IF CELERY GETS ALL NOODLEY BEFORE YOU FINISH THE BAG, BUY IT ONLY AS YOU NEED IT.

ON THE OTHER HAND, SOME REFRIGERATED FOODS THAT YOU USE FAIRLY OFTEN, SUCH AS CHEESES, ARE CONSIDERED STAPLES. CHEESES THAT KEEP WELL IN THE REFRIGERATOR INCLUDE PARMESAN AND ROMANO. SOME FREQUENTLY USED SOFT CHEESES, SUCH AS MOZZARELLA AND CHEDDAR, MAY ALSO BE CONSIDERED STAPLES IF YOU USE THEM SO FREQUENTLY THEY DON'T HAVE A CHANCE TO SPOIL.

THE FREEZER IS AN EXCELLENT PLACE FOR PANTRY ITEMS. OFTEN-USED MEATS, SUCH AS CHICKEN BREASTS AND BACON, CAN BE STORED FOR SHORT PERIODS OF TIME IN THE FREEZER. OTHER FOODS, LIKE FLOUR AND NUTS, WILL KEEP LONGER IF STORED IN THE FREEZER.

HERBS AND SPICES

STORE DRIED HERBS AND SPICES IN A COOL, DRY PLACE (NOT ABOVE THE STOVE) TO KEEP THEM AT THEIR PEAK OF FLAVOR. THEY WILL LOSE MUCH OF THEIR FLAVOR AFTER A YEAR, SO BUY SMALL CONTAINERS. **WRITE THE DATE YOU OPENED THEM ON THE LABEL.**

LIQUEURS AND WINES

FLAVORED LIQUEURS HAVE HIGHLY CONCENTRATED FLAVORS, MAKING THEM A GREAT COOKING STAPLE. **STORED IN A COOL, DARK PLACE, THEY LAST ALMOST INDEFINITELY.** BUY SMALL BOTTLES, THOUGH, ESPECIALLY WHEN BUYING SOMETHING NEW TO YOU. WINES ALSO CONTRIBUTE A RICH AND SUBTLE FLAVOR TO RECIPES. **STORE WINE BOTTLES ON THEIR SIDES IN A COOL, DARK PLACE.**

PANTRY ITEMS

Baking powder
Baking soda
Beans, canned (black, garbanzo, Mexican-style chili, white)
Bread crumbs (dry)
Broth or bouillon (beef, chicken, vegetable)
Bulgur
Cake and brownie mixes
Catsup
Chocolate-flavored syrup
Chocolate (semisweet pieces, bars, white baking bar, white pieces)
Coffee (instant crystals, instant espresso powder)
Corn, canned (baby, cream-style, whole kernel, whole kernel with sweet pepper)
Cornmeal, yellow
Cornstarch
Dressings (honey-mustard, Italian, vinaigrettes)
Dried fruit (apricots, blueberries, cherries, cranberries, figs, mixed fruit bits, raisins)
Flour (all-purpose white)
Fruit, canned (pears)
Garlic (bulb, bottled)
Graham crackers (crumbs)
Green chiles (canned, diced)
Hot pepper sauce
Maple syrup
Microwave popcorn
Milk (evaporated skim, sweetened condensed)
Miniature phyllo shells
Mustard (Dijon-style, honey, spicy brown, yellow)
Nonstick spray coating

Nuts (almonds, cashews, dry roasted peanuts, pecans, walnuts)
Oats (quick-cooking, rolled)
Oils (olive, roasted garlic, vegetable)
Olives (green, kalamata, ripe)
Onions (green, red, yellow)
Pasta, dried (bow tie, orzo/rosamarina, ramen noodles, shells, tortellini)
Pie fillings (apple, cherry)
Potatoes (red, russet, yellow)
Preserves (strawberry)
Pudding (instant mix)
Rice (brown, instant, long grain white, pilaf mixes)
Salsa
Soy sauce
Spaghetti sauce
Strawberry ice cream topping
Sugar (brown, granulated, powdered)
Tomatoes, canned (Italian-style stewed, stewed, tomato sauce)
Tomatoes, dried (dried, oil-pack)
Tomatoes, fresh (common, roma)
Tortilla chips
Tortillas (flour)
Tuna, canned
Vinegar (balsamic, red wine, white balsamic, white wine)
Worcestershire sauce

REFRIGERATED & FROZEN ITEMS

Butter
Capers
Carrots
Celery
Cherries (maraschino)
Chicken (breasts; chopped, cooked chicken; cooked, cubed chicken)
Eggs
Frozen puff pastry
Fruit, frozen (blueberries, raspberries, rhubarb, strawberries)
Lemon juice
Lime juice
Mango chutney
Margarine
Mayonnaise
Milk
Orange juice
Pita bread
Vegetables, frozen (broccoli, carrots, cauliflower, green beans, mixed, pea pods, spinach)

HERBS AND SPICES

Almond extract
Cardamom
Chili powder
Cinnamon, ground
Cloves, ground
Cumin, ground
Curry powder
Garlic pepper
Garlic salt
Ginger, ground
Herb-pepper seasoning
Jamaican jerk seasoning
Marjoram leaves
Mustard, dry
Nutmeg, ground
Onion powder
Oregano leaves
Paprika
Pepper (black, ground red, crushed red flakes)
Rosemary leaves
Sage leaves
Salt

Sesame seed
Tarragon leaves
Thyme leaves
Vanilla extract

LIQUORS

Almond-flavored liqueur (Amaretto)
Coffee-flavored liqueur (Crème de Cacao)
Currant-flavored liqueur (Crème de Cassis)
Orange-flavored liqueur (Grand Marnier)
Sherry, dry
Wines (dry red, dry white)

THE FOLLOWING ITEMS AREN'T USED IN THE BOOK, BUT ARE GOOD ADDITIONS TO A BASIC PANTRY. STOCK THEM IF YOU WISH

Basil leaves
Bay leaves
Cocoa, unsweetened
Corn syrup (light and dark)
Cream of tartar
Flour (whole wheat)
Garlic powder
Honey
Molasses
Mustard seed
Oils (peanut)
Pasta (angel hair, fettucine, macaroni, spaghetti)
Peanut butter
Pepper (white)
Rice (converted, wild)
Tomatoes, canned (diced, tomato paste, whole roma)
Vegetables, frozen (corn)
Vinegar (cider, distilled white, rice wine)
Port wine
Yeast, active dry

Adventures in Appetizers

Tomato & Olive Salsa

WITH RIPE ROMAS, GOOD BLACK OLIVES, AND A HEALTHY DOSE OF FRESH BASIL, YOU'LL BE TEMPTED TO SKIP THE CHIPS AND EAT THIS WITH A SPOON.

INGREDIENTS

Makes about 2½ cups
Start to finish: 15 min.

- 6 roma tomatoes, quartered lengthwise
- ½ cup sliced pitted ripe olives
- 1 small red onion, cut up
- ½ cup lightly packed fresh basil leaves
- 2 tablespoons olive oil
- 1 tablespoon red wine vinegar
- ¼ teaspoon salt
  Toasted Pita chips (see tip, page 17)

✓ *Grocery List*
FRESH BASIL

DIRECTIONS

1. In a food processor bowl combine tomatoes, olives, onion, basil, olive oil, vinegar, and salt. Cover and process with several on-off turns until finely chopped. (Or, finely chop the tomatoes, olives, onion, and basil; stir in the olive oil and vinegar.) Serve immediately with pita chips.

NOTE: If you like goat cheese, sprinkle ½ cup crumbled goat cheese on top of the mixture (do not stir in) for extra flavor.

NUTRITION FACTS PER TABLESPOON SALSA: 10 calories, 1 g total fat (0 g saturated fat), 0 mg cholesterol, 23 mg sodium, 1 g carbohydrate, 0 g fiber, 0 g protein. Daily Values: 0% vit. A, 2% vit. C, 0% calcium, 0% iron.

Greek-Style Spanakopita dip

with Pita Chips

PLAIN PITA CHIPS PARTNER WELL WITH THE BOLD FLAVORS OF THIS SPICY DIP—IT'S A LOVE-FEST OF FLAVORS JUST WAITING TO HAPPEN.

INGREDIENTS

Makes about 3 cups

Prep: 15 min. Bake: 10 min. (chips)

- 1   15-ounce carton whole-milk ricotta cheese
- 1   6-ounce carton plain low-fat or fat-free yogurt
- ½   of a 10-ounce package frozen chopped spinach, thawed and well drained
- ⅓   cup crumbled garlic-and-herb feta cheese
- 1   4½-ounce can chopped pitted ripe olives
- ¼   cup sliced green onions
- 1   to 2 cloves garlic, minced
- ½   teaspoon salt
- ⅛   teaspoon pepper
- 1   recipe Pita Chips (see tip, page 17)

✓ *Grocery List*
   RICOTTA CHEESE
   PLAIN YOGURT
   FETA CHEESE

DIRECTIONS

*1.*In a medium mixing bowl beat ricotta cheese and yogurt with an electric mixer until smooth. Stir in drained spinach, feta cheese, olives, green onions, garlic, salt, and pepper. Cover and refrigerate up to 24 hours. Serve with Pita Chips.

WHAT HE **LONGED** TO HEAR...

TRY SPOONING THE DIP INTO ASSORTED-COLOR PEPPER HALVES AND SERVE PITA CHIPS AROUND THE PEPPERS... *THEY'LL LOVE IT!*

NUTRITION FACTS PER TABLESPOON DIP: 27 calories, 2 g total fat (1 g saturated fat), 6 mg cholesterol, 71 mg sodium, 1 g carbohydrate, 0 g fiber, 2 g protein. Daily Values: 3% vit. A, 0% vit. C, 3% calcium, 0% iron.

15

Zesty Black Bean Dip

AFTER A SPIN IN THE FOOD PROCESSOR, A LOWLY CAN OF BLACK BEANS MIRACULOUSLY MORPHS INTO A CHIP DIP WITH PLENTY OF TANG.

INGREDIENTS

Makes about 2½ cups
Start to finish: 10 min.

- 2 15-ounce cans black beans, rinsed and drained
- ⅓ cup salsa
- 2 tablespoons lime juice
- ½ teaspoon bottled minced garlic
- ¼ teaspoon salt
- 1 cup finely chopped tomatoes
   Finely chopped green onion (optional)
   Tortilla chips or pita chips

✓ *"Pantry Only... no shopping required!"*

DIRECTIONS

1. In a food processor bowl or blender container combine beans, salsa, lime juice, garlic, and salt. Cover and process or blend until nearly smooth. To serve, top with tomatoes and, if desired, green onion. Serve with tortilla chips.

CREAMY ZESTY BLACK BEAN DIP: Prepare as above, except add one 3-ounce package softened cream cheese to the mixture before processing or blending.

NUTRITION FACTS PER TABLESPOON DIP: 16 calories, 0 g total fat (0 g saturated fat), 0 mg cholesterol, 74 mg sodium, 3 g carbohydrate, 1 g fiber, 1 g protein. Daily Values: 0% vit. A, 3% vit. C, 0% calcium, 1% iron.

Hummus

YOU **COULD** BUY THE READY-MADE STUFF, BUT WHY SCHLEP TO THE STORE WHEN YOU CAN WHIR IT UP FRESH—ANYTIME—WITH ITEMS YOU KEEP ON HAND?

INGREDIENTS

MAKES 1¾ cups
Prep: 10 min. **Bake:** 10 min. (chips)

- 1   15-ounce can chickpeas (garbanzo beans), undrained
- ¼   cup tahini (sesame paste)
- 1   tablespoon lemon juice
- 2   to 4 cloves garlic
- ¼   teaspoon salt
- ¼   to ½ teaspoon ground red pepper (optional)

  Pita chips (see tip, right) and/or assorted vegetable dippers

✓ *Add tahini to your pantry, and this, too, will be a Pantry Only recipe, with no shopping required!*

DIRECTIONS

1. In a food processor bowl or blender container combine undrained chickpeas, tahini, lemon juice, garlic, salt, and, if desired, ground red pepper. Cover and process or blend until smooth. Serve with pita bread wedges, pita crisps, bagel chips, carrot sticks, and/or celery sticks.

PITA CHIPS A.S.A.P!!!

BREAD GETS STALE, CRACKERS GO SOGGY—BUT **PITA CHIPS** HAVE TO BE ONE OF THE MOST VERSATILE, EASY-TO-KEEP-ON-HAND APPETIZER BREADS. KEEP A BUNCH OF PITA BREAD IN THE FRIDGE OR FREEZER, AND YOU CAN TOAST AS NEEDED.
HERE'S HOW:

SPLIT 4 PITA BREAD ROUNDS IN HALF HORIZONTALLY; CUT EACH HALF INTO 6 WEDGES. PLACE WEDGES IN A SINGLE LAYER ON TWO COOKIE SHEETS. BAKE IN A 350° OVEN ABOUT 10 MINUTES OR UNTIL CRISP AND LIGHTLY BROWNED. STORE IN AN AIRTIGHT CONTAINER AT ROOM TEMPERATURE UP TO FOUR DAYS. FREEZE UP TO 3 WEEKS. **MAKES 48 CHIPS.**

NUTRITION FACTS PER ¼ CUP SPREAD: 25 calories, 1 g total fat (0 g saturated fat), 0 mg cholesterol, 72 mg sodium, 3 g carbohydrate, 1 g fiber, 1 g protein. Daily Values: 0% vit. A, 1% vit. C, 0% calcium, 2% iron.

Portobello Pizzettas

IN BOTH SIZE AND MEATY TEXTURE, THE MIGHTY PORTOBELLO IS THE KING OF MUSHROOMS. A QUICK BROIL UNLOCKS ITS JUICY GOODNESS.

INGREDIENTS

Makes 12 pizzettas

Prep: 10 min. **Bake:** 12 min.

- ½ of a 10-ounce package frozen chopped spinach, thawed and well drained
- 1½ cups shredded mozzarella cheese (6 ounces)
- ½ cup coarsely chopped turkey pepperoni or pepperoni
- 1 teaspoon dried basil, crushed
- ¼ teaspoon coarsely ground pepper
- 12 fresh portobello mushrooms (3 to 4 inches in diameter)
- 2 tablespoons margarine, melted
  Fresh basil (optional)

✓ *Grocery List*
**TURKEY PEPPERONI
MOZZARELLA CHEESE
PORTOBELLO MUSHROOMS**

DIRECTIONS

1. Finely chop the spinach. In a mixing bowl combine spinach, cheese, pepperoni, basil, and pepper; set aside. Clean mushrooms; remove stems. Place open side up on a lightly greased cookie sheet; brush with margarine. Spoon 2 tablespoons spinach mixture into each.

2. Bake in a 350° oven about 12 minutes or until heated through. (Or, place mushrooms on the unheated rack of a broiler pan. Broil 4 inches from the heat for 3 to 4 minutes.) If desired, garnish with fresh basil.

NUTRITION FACTS PER SERVING: 78 calories, 5 g total fat (2 g saturated fat), 16 mg cholesterol, 201 mg sodium, 2 g carbohydrate, 1 g fiber, 6 g protein. Daily Values: 10% vit. A, 3% vit. C, 8% calcium, 5% iron.

Nutty Olive Quesadillas

What's better than melting cheese? Melting two kinds of cheese in tortillas to create a twist on a favorite Mexican appetizer.

INGREDIENTS

Makes 6 servings
Prep: 15 min. **Cook:** 4 min.

- 6 6-inch flour or corn tortillas
- 1 cup shredded mozzarella cheese (4 ounces)
- ⅔ cup crumbled feta cheese
- ¼ cup chopped walnuts
- ¼ cup chopped pitted ripe olives
- 2 teaspoons snipped fresh oregano or ½ teaspoon dried oregano, crushed
- 1 tablespoon olive oil
   Salsa

✓ *Grocery List*
   MOZZARELLA CHEESE
   FETA CHEESE
   FRESH OREGANO

DIRECTIONS

1. To soften tortillas, wrap in foil; heat in a 350° oven for 10 minutes. Meanwhile, combine mozzarella cheese, feta cheese, nuts, olives, and oregano; spread over half of each tortilla. Fold in half; secure with toothpicks. Brush one side with some of the olive oil.

2. In a large skillet cook tortillas, oil side down, over medium-low heat for 4 minutes, brushing with oil and turning once. Cut into triangles. Serve with salsa.

THERE'S ONE IN EVERY CROWD...

CALIFORNIA RIPE OLIVES ARE THE EASIEST TO FIND AND, BECAUSE THEY'RE OFTEN PITTED, THE EASIEST TO USE. HOWEVER, IF YOU (OR ONE OF YOUR GUESTS) IS AN "OLIVE SNOB," YOU MIGHT WANT TO SUBSTITUTE THE IMPORTED VARIETIES, SUCH AS KALAMATA OR NIÇOISE. BUT REMEMBER, YOU'LL HAVE TO PIT THEM YOURSELF—THOUGH IF YOU LOOK HARD ENOUGH, YOU MAY FIND PITTED KALAMATA OLIVES IN SOME ITALIAN SPECIALTY STORES.

NUTRITION FACTS PER SERVING: 239 calories, 14 g total fat (5 g saturated fat), 23 mg cholesterol, 297 mg sodium, 1 g fiber, 20 g carbohydrate, 10 g protein. Daily Values: 7% vit. A, 0% vit. C, 31% calcium, 11% iron.

BLT Bruschetta

ANY HAPPENING BRUSCHETTA BOASTS GARLIC GALORE, BUT IF YOU REALLY WANT TO GET THESE TOASTY GEMS NOTICED, BRING ON THE BACON.

INGREDIENTS

Makes 16 bruschetta
Start to finish: 15 min.

16 ½-inch-thick slices baguette-style French bread, toasted
½ cup semisoft cheese with garlic and herb
½ cup very thinly sliced fresh basil leaves or shredded leaf lettuce
½ cup chopped tomato
4 slices bacon, crisp-cooked, drained, and crumbled, or 4 ounces pancetta, cooked, drained, and chopped

✓ *Grocery List*
FRENCH BREAD BAGUETTE
SEMISOFT CHEESE WITH GARLIC AND HERB
FRESH BASIL
BACON

DIRECTIONS

1. Spread one side of each toast slice with cheese. Top with basil, tomato, and bacon. Serve immediately.

WITH SOPHISTICATED GUESTS ON THEIR WAY, **SHE SUDDENLY RECALLED...**

IT WILL BE ALL RIGHT—KEEPING THAT BAGUETTE IN THE FREEZER WAS A GOOD MOVE! NOW ALL I HAVE TO DO IS CUT IT INTO ROUNDS, TOAST IT, AND TOP WITH JUST ABOUT ANYTHING.... FRESH MOZZARELLA, FETA-PLUS OLIVES, FRESH BASIL, PARSLEY, AND ROSEMARY (WELL, I SUPPOSE DRIED HERBS WILL DO IN A PINCH)...I'LL DRIZZLE IT ALL WITH EXTRA-VIRGIN OLIVE OIL. THEY'LL THINK I'M SO... CONTINENTAL!

NUTRITION FACTS PER SERVING: 75 calories, 4 g total fat (2 g saturated fat), 8 mg cholesterol, 112 mg sodium, 8 g carbohydrate, 0 g fiber, 2 g protein. Daily Values: 1% vit. A, 3% vit. C, 1% calcium, 2% iron.

Fresh Mozzarella
with Basil

FRESH MOZZARELLA IS CREAMY AND MORE DELICATE THAN PACKAGED MOZZARELLAS, LENDING THAT CERTAIN "JE NE SAIS QUOI" TO THIS DISH.

INGREDIENTS

Makes 14 to 16 servings
Start to finish: 15 min.

- 16 ounces fresh mozzarella cheese
- ¼ cup roasted garlic oil or olive oil
- 2 tablespoons snipped fresh basil or 1 teaspoon dried basil, crushed
- 1 tablespoon cracked pepper
- 1 to 2 teaspoons balsamic vinegar
  Baguette slices (optional)

✓ *Grocery List*
FRESH MOZZARELLA
FRESH BASIL
FRENCH BAGUETTE

DIRECTIONS

1. Cut mozzarella into 1-inch cubes; place in a medium bowl. Add oil, basil, pepper, and vinegar; toss gently until cheese is well coated with oil and seasonings. Serve immediately. (Or, refrigerate, covered, for several days.) Spear cheese with toothpicks and, if desired, serve with baguette slices.

NUTRITION FACTS PER SERVING: 100 calories, 7 g total fat (4 g saturated fat), 18 mg cholesterol, 151 mg sodium, 1 g carbohydrate, 0 g fiber, 8 g protein. Daily Values: 5% vit. A, 0% vit. C, 17% calcium, 0% iron

Zucchini Canapés

ZUCCHINI SOMETIMES GETS A BUM RAP AS BEING MORE GOOD FOR YOU THAN GOOD TO EAT. THIS SPREAD PUTS AN END TO SUCH UGLY RUMORS.

INGREDIENTS

Makes 36 canapés

Start to finish: 20 min.

- 1 medium to large zucchini, cut into ¼-inch-thick slices
- ½ of an 8-ounce tub (⅓ cup) cream cheese with salmon or ⅓ cup semisoft cheese with garlic and herb
- 1 tablespoon sliced or chopped pitted ripe olives
- 1 tablespoon snipped fresh chives

✓ *Grocery List*

ZUCCHINI
CREAM CHEESE
FRESH CHIVES

DIRECTIONS

1. Pat the zucchini slices dry with paper towels. Spread desired cream cheese over zucchini slices. Sprinkle each with olives and chives. Serve immediately. (Or, refrigerate, covered, for 1 to 2 hours.)

JANE KEPT UP **APPEARANCES!**

IT'S ALWAYS GOOD TO HAVE AN ASSORTMENT OF NIBBLES. BUT WHO HAS TIME FOR THAT? I'LL JUST MAKE ONE STARTER FROM SCRATCH AND FILL OUT MY APPETIZER TRAY WITH FUN BITES FROM THE ITALIAN IMPORT STORE—IMPORTED MEATS AND CHEESES, BREADS, OLIVES, ROASTED RED PEPPERS—IT WILL LOOK SO WORLDLY AND WONDERFUL, WITHOUT THE WORK!

NUTRITION FACTS PER CANAPÉ: 12 calories, 1 g total fat (1 g saturated fat), 3 mg cholesterol, 27 mg sodium, 1 g carbohydrate, 0 g fiber, 0 g protein. Daily Values: 1% vit. A, 2% vit. C, 1% calcium, 0% iron.

Quick Focaccia Breadsticks

TRUE STORY! IN AN INCREDIBLE 15 MINUTES YOUR GUESTS CAN REVEL IN HOT BREADSTICKS WITH OIL-PACKED TOMATOES AND FRESH ROSEMARY.

INGREDIENTS

Makes 10 breadsticks

Prep: 15 min. **Bake:** 12 min.

- ¼ cup oil-packed dried tomatoes
- ¼ cup grated Romano cheese
- 2 teaspoons water
- 1½ teaspoons snipped fresh rosemary or ½ teaspoon dried rosemary, crushed
- ⅛ teaspoon cracked black pepper
- 1 10-ounce package refrigerated pizza dough

✓ *Grocery List*

ROMANO CHEESE
FRESH ROSEMARY
REFRIGERATED PIZZA DOUGH

DIRECTIONS

1. Drain dried tomatoes, reserving oil; finely snip tomatoes. In a mixing bowl combine tomatoes, 2 teaspoons of the reserved oil, cheese, water, rosemary, and pepper. Set aside.

2. Unroll pizza dough. On a lightly floured surface, roll the dough into a 10×8-inch rectangle. Spread the tomato mixture crosswise over half of the dough.

3. Fold plain half of dough over filling; press lightly. Cut folded dough lengthwise into ten ½-inch strips. Fold each strip in half and twist two or three times. Place 1 inch apart on a lightly greased baking sheet.

4. Bake in a 350° oven for 12 to 15 minutes or until golden brown. Cool on a wire rack.

NUTRITION FACTS PER BREADSTICK: 113 calories, 3 g total fat (1 g saturated fat), 3 mg cholesterol, 263 mg sodium, 18 g carbohydrate, 1 g fiber, 5 g protein. Daily Values: 1% vit. A, 5% vit. C, 3% calcium, 5% iron.

23

Savory Nut Mix

AT THE END OF A TRYING DAY, THE AROMA OF TOASTING NUTS SEEMS TO MAKE EVERYTHING RIGHT IN THE WORLD. PAIR THIS WITH YOUR FAVORITE SIPPER.

INGREDIENTS

Makes 2 cups
Prep: 10 min. **Bake:** 12 min.

- 2 tablespoons white wine Worcestershire sauce
- 1 tablespoon olive oil
- 2 teaspoons snipped fresh thyme or ½ teaspoon dried thyme, crushed
- 1 teaspoon snipped fresh rosemary or ¼ teaspoon dried rosemary, crushed
- ¼ teaspoon salt
- ⅛ teaspoon ground red pepper
- 2 cups macadamia nuts and/or walnuts

✓ Grocery List

FRESH THYME AND ROSEMARY
MACADAMIA NUTS

DIRECTIONS

1. Combine Worcestershire sauce, olive oil, thyme, rosemary, salt, and ground red pepper. Spread nuts in a 13×9×2-inch baking pan. Drizzle with oil mixture; toss gently to coat. Bake in a 350° oven for 12 to 15 minutes or until nuts are toasted, stirring occasionally. Spread onto foil; cool. Store in an airtight container. Garnish serving dish with a sprig of fresh thyme.

LESSONS LEARNED **THE HARD WAY!!!**

I HATE IT WHEN GOOD THINGS GO BAD! NEXT TIME, I'LL KEEP ITEMS USED INFREQUENTLY (SUCH AS NUTS AND FLOUR) IN THE REFRIGERATOR OR FREEZER IN AIRTIGHT CONTAINERS.

NUTRITION FACTS PER ¼ CUP SERVING: 253 calories, 26 g total fat (4 g saturated fat), 0 mg cholesterol, 100 mg sodium, 5 g carbohydrate, 3 g fiber, 3 g protein. Daily values: 0% vit. A, 0% vit. C, 2% calcium, 5% iron.

White Chocolate
Popcorn, Pretzels, & Peanuts

WHITE CHOCOLATE ISN'T REALLY CHOCOLATE (IT LACKS THE REQUISITE LIQUOR). BUT ITS RICH TASTE WILL PLACATE EVEN THE FRAUD POLICE.

INGREDIENTS

Makes about 16 cups

Start to finish: 10 min.

- 1 3½-ounce bag plain white microwave popcorn, popped (about 8 cups)
- 2 cups miniature pretzel twists
- 1 cup dry roasted peanuts
- ½ cup snipped dried apricots, cherries, or cranberries; raisins; or candy-coated chocolate pieces
- 1 12-ounce package white baking pieces

✓ *Grocery List*

MINIATURE PRETZEL TWISTS

DIRECTIONS

1. In a very large bowl combine popcorn, pretzels, peanuts, and apricots; set aside.

2. Place baking pieces in a microwave-safe bowl. Microcook, uncovered, on 100 percent power (high) for 1 minute; stir. Continue to microcook at 30 second intervals until melted. Pour melted pieces over popcorn mixture, tossing to coat. Spoon mixture onto waxed paper. Cool completely.

NUTRITION FACTS PER 1/2 CUP: 110 calories, 6 g total fat (3 g saturated fat), 4 mg cholesterol, 96 mg sodium, 12 g carbohydrate, 1 g fiber, 2 g protein. Daily Values: 1% vit. A, 0% vit. C, 1% calcium, 1% iron.

DIAL "S" for Sandwich

EGGPLANT & GOUDA Sandwich

EGGPLANT IS THE MASTER OF DISGUISES, TAKING ON WHATEVER FLAVORS IT ENCOUNTERS. HERE, GOUDA GIVES IT A DISTINCTIVE DUTCH COVER.

INGREDIENTS

Makes 4 sandwiches

Prep: 15 min. **Cook:** 1 min.

- 8 ½-inch-thick slices sourdough bread
- ½ of a small eggplant, peeled, if desired (about 6 oz.)
- 1 clove garlic, minced
- 1 to 2 tablespoons cooking oil
- ¼ cup mayonnaise or salad dressing
- 4 lettuce leaves
- 4 1-ounce slices Gouda cheese
- 1 small tomato, sliced

✓ *Grocery List*
  - *EGGPLANT*
  - *GOUDA CHEESE*
  - *LETTUCE*
  - *SOURDOUGH BREAD*

DIRECTIONS

1. Toast sourdough bread slices; set aside. Meanwhile, cut eggplant into ½-inch-thick slices. In a large skillet cook garlic in hot oil for 30 seconds. Add eggplant slices. Cook about 4 minutes or until eggplant is tender, turning once. Drain the eggplant slices on paper towels.

2. For each sandwich, divide 1 tablespoon of mayonnaise between 2 toasted bread slices, spreading evenly. With mayonnaise side up, top 1 bread slice with one-fourth of lettuce, cheese, eggplant, and tomato. Sprinkle with salt and pepper. Add remaining bread slice, mayonnaise side down.

NUTRITION FACTS PER SANDWICH: 387 calories, 24 g total fat (8 g saturated fat), 40 mg cholesterol, 656 mg sodium, 31 g carbohydrate, 2 g fiber, 12 g protein. Daily Values: 8% vit. A, 9% vit. C, 20% calcium, 11% iron.

NIÇOISE TUNA Sandwich

NO LONGER HOPELESSY BLASÉ, THIS TUNA SALAD GETS A CHIC MAKEOVER. WHAT A DIFFERENCE CAPERS OR OLIVES MAKE!

INGREDIENTS

Makes 4 sandwiches
Start to finish: 20 min.

- ¼ cup finely chopped onion
- 1 to 1½ tablespoons lemon juice
- 1 tablespoon olive oil
- 1 tablespoon sliced pitted ripe olives or drained capers
- 1 garlic clove, minced
- 1 12-ounce can tuna (water pack), well drained and broken into chunks
- 4 sourdough rolls (8 ounces) or one 8-ounce loaf baguette-style French bread, cut into quarters
- 2 plum tomatoes, sliced
- 1⅓ cups shredded lettuce or torn mixed salad greens

✓ Grocery List
    LETTUCE
    SOURDOUGH ROLLS

DIRECTIONS

1. In a medium bowl stir together onion, lemon juice, olive oil, olives, and garlic. Gently stir in the tuna.

2. Split rolls or bread lengthwise; fill with tuna mixture. Top with tomatoes and lettuce.

YOU JET-SETTER, YOU!

WHEN SERVING THIS SANDWICH TO FRIENDS, YOU **COULD** CALL IT NIÇOISE TUNA SANDWICH—BUT IF YOU REALLY WANT TO TURN HEADS, TELL THEM IT'S A **PAN BAGNAT!** THIS SPECIALTY OF NICE—OFTEN ENJOYED ALONG ROMANTIC LITTLE BEACHFRONT CAFES ON THE **FRENCH RIVIERA**—IS BASICALLY THE SAME SANDWICH...WELL, EXCEPT THAT THE FRENCH MIGHT ADD SOME HARD-BOILED EGG SLICES, AND MAYBE SOME ANCHOVIES...BUT HOW MANY OF YOUR FRIENDS WILL KNOW THAT? (P.S. IT'S PRONOUNCED PAN BANYA.)

NUTRITION FACTS PER SANDWICH: 271 calories, 5 g total fat (1 g saturated fat), 10 mg cholesterol, 384 mg sodium, 37 g carbohydrate, 1 g fiber, 21 g protein. Daily Values: 3% vit. A, 14% vit. C, 1% calcium, 16% iron.

ANTIPASTO
Sandwich

Ciao bella! Diners in Rome would likely fall in love with this sandwich, so long as you didn't tell them the bread is French!

INGREDIENTS

Makes 4 sandwiches
Prep: 15 min. **Cook:** 1 min.

- 4 6-inch French-style rolls, split
- 3 ounces thinly sliced cooked ham
- 1 6½-ounce jar marinated artichoke hearts, drained, or one 7-ounce jar roasted red sweet peppers, drained
- 4 slices fresh mozzarella cheese or fontina cheese (about 4 ounces)
- 4 thin slices red onion, separated into rings
- ¼ cup bottled Italian salad dressing
- 4 lettuce leaves

✓ *Grocery List*
  MOZZARELLA CHEESE
  FRENCH-STYLE ROLLS
  HAM
  LETTUCE

DIRECTIONS

1. Layer bottom halves of rolls with ham, artichoke hearts or red sweet peppers, and cheese. Place on a cookie sheet along with roll tops, cut sides up. Broil 3 to 4 inches from the heat for 1 to 2 minutes or until roll tops are toasted and cheese is melted. Top with onion; drizzle with salad dressing. Finish with lettuce and roll tops.

WHAT IS *ANTIPASTO?!*

IF ANYONE TRIES TO TELL YOU THAT ANTIPASTO MEANS "BEFORE THE PASTA," TELL THEM THEY'RE **WRONG! WRONG!** ANTIPASTO IS AN ITALIAN WORD MEANING "BEFORE THE MEAL." IT REFERS TO AN ASSORTMENT OF **HOT OR COLD APPETIZERS** COMMONLY SERVED AS A FIRST COURSE BEFORE AN ITALIAN MEAL. THIS ARRAY OF WELL-SEASONED, SAVORY FOODS INCLUDES ITALIAN CURED MEATS, CHEESES, PICKLED OR MARINATED VEGETABLES, AND CANNED, PICKLED, OR CURED FISH.

NUTRITION FACTS PER SANDWICH: 370 calories, 18 g total fat (5 g saturated fat), 27 mg cholesterol, 984 mg sodium, 37 g carbohydrate, 0 g fiber, 17 g protein. Daily Values: 9% vit. A, 26% vit. C, 21% calcium, 15% iron.

PINEAPPLE CREAM CHEESE Sandwiches

FRUITED CREAM CHEESE LENDS A SUBLIME LAYER OF SWEETNESS TO THIS SANDWICH, MAKING IT A SEDUCTIVE LITTLE NUMBER INDEED.

INGREDIENTS

Makes 12 sandwiches

Start to finish: 25 min.

- 3 medium carrots
- ⅓ cup dried cranberries, raisins, or mixed dried fruit bits
- ¼ cup shelled sunflower seeds
- 6 6- or 7-inch Italian bread shells (Boboli) or Italian flatbreads (focaccia)
- 2 8-ounce tubs cream cheese with pineapple

✓ *Grocery List*

SUNFLOWER SEEDS
ITALIAN BREAD SHELLS
PINEAPPLE CREAM CHEESE

DIRECTIONS

1. Peel carrots. Carefully cut carrots into long, thin ribbons with a vegetable peeler. Place carrot ribbons in cold water to crisp. Set aside.

2. Combine cranberries, raisins, or mixed dried fruit bits and sunflower seeds. Slice bread shells in half horizontally. For each sandwich, spread cream cheese on both cut sides of bread. Sprinkle fruit mixture onto cream cheese. Add carrot ribbons. Top with remaining half of bread. Slice sandwiches in half. Serve immediately. (Or, wrap sandwiches in plastic wrap; refrigerate up to 24 hours.)

NUTRITION FACTS PER SANDWICH: 307 calories, 16 g total fat (7 g saturated fat), 36 mg cholesterol, 455 mg sodium, 34 g carbohydrate, 2 g fiber, 9 g protein. Daily Values: 58% vit. A, 2% vit. C, 7% calcium, 9% iron.

FISH FILLET
Muffuletta

THE ORIGINAL MUFFULETTA FEATURED SALAMI. HERE, BREADED FISH BRINGS THAT COMFORT-FOOD TOUCH TO THE NEW ORLEANS SPECIALTY.

INGREDIENTS

Makes 4 muffulettas

Start to finish: 25 min.

- 4 frozen battered or breaded fish fillets
- 3 tablespoons mayonnaise or salad dressing
- 1 teaspoon finely shredded lime peel
- 2 teaspoons lime juice
- 1 cup packaged shredded cabbage with carrot (cole slaw mix) or shredded cabbage
- 4 3½- to 4-inch French-style or club rolls, split
- ½ cup salsa
- ½ cup sliced pitted Greek black olives
- 2 tablespoons capers, drained

✓ Grocery List

FROZEN FISH FILLETS
LIMES
COLESLAW MIX
FRENCH-STYLE ROLLS

DIRECTIONS

1. Cook fish according to package directions. Meanwhile, in a medium bowl stir together mayonnaise, lime peel, and lime juice. Add cabbage; stir until combined. Set aside. Hollow out the inside of top halves of each roll, leaving a ½-inch-thick shell. Place a fish fillet on the bottom half of each roll. Top with cabbage mixture and salsa. Sprinkle with olives and capers. Top with bread tops.

NUTRITION FACTS PER MUFFULETTA: 457 calories, 25 g total fat (3 g saturated fat), 26 mg cholesterol, 1,123 mg sodium, 46 g carbohydrate, 1 g fiber, 14 g protein. Daily Values: 24% vit. A, 31% vit. C, 5% calcium, 15% iron.

TOASTED PASTRAMI Sandwiches

ONE TASTE OF THIS OOZY BEAUTY, AND ANY CONCERNS YOU HAVE ABOUT COMBINING ALL THESE FLAVORS AND TEXTURES WILL MELT AWAY.

INGREDIENTS

Makes 4 sandwiches
Prep: 20 min. **Bake:** 15 min.

- 1 large onion, thinly sliced and separated into rings
- 1 medium green sweet pepper, cut into thin strips
- ⅓ cup bottled reduced-calorie clear Italian salad dressing
- 4 4-inch French-style rolls, split
- 8 slices cooked turkey pastrami (8 ounces)
- 2 ounces thinly sliced provolone or Swiss cheese
- 3 plum tomatoes, thinly sliced
- 4 teaspoons tarragon mustard or peppercorn mustard

✓ Grocery List

GREEN SWEET PEPPER
FRENCH-STYLE ROLLS
TURKEY PASTRAMI
PROVOLONE OR SWISS CHEESE
TARRAGON MUSTARD

DIRECTIONS

1. In an 8-inch skillet cook onion and sweet pepper in salad dressing until tender. Remove the skillet from heat.

2. For each sandwich, place the bottom of a roll on a 12-inch square of foil. Top with turkey pastrami, cheese, and tomato slices. Spoon on the onion-sweet pepper mixture, including any remaining dressing. Spread cut side of the roll top with mustard; place atop the fillings. Wrap each sandwich in the foil, sealing the ends.

3. Heat sandwiches in a 350° oven for 15 to 20 minutes or until cheese is melted. Serve warm.

NOONTIME NO-BRAINER!!!

SOME THINGS ARE ABOVE INNOVATION, HONEY!

YOU'RE RIGHT—WHAT BETTER WAY TO SERVE THIS GREAT SANDWICH THAN ALONGSIDE A LITTLE PASTA SALAD AND A PILE OF POTATO CHIPS?

NUTRITION FACTS PER SANDWICH: 355 calories, 12 g total fat (4 g saturated fat), 11 mg cholesterol, 1,254 mg sodium, 40 g carbohydrate, 2 g fiber, 21 g protein. Daily Values: 6% vit. A, 36% vit. C, 15% calcium, 22% iron.

TURKEY & PESTO
Pita Pockets

TIRED OF HO-HUM TURKEY AND MAYO? ADD A LITTLE "PESTO CHANGE-O" TO THE ROUTINE WITH A VEGGIE-STUDDED BASIL-PESTO SPREAD.

INGREDIENTS

Makes 4 sandwiches
Start to finish: 15 min.

- 2 cups chopped cooked turkey breast
- 1 cup shredded Swiss cheese (4 ounces)
- ¼ cup finely chopped celery
- ¼ cup shredded carrot
- ¼ cup mayonnaise or salad dressing
- ¼ cup prepared basil pesto
- 4 pita bread rounds, halved crosswise
- 1 cup shredded lettuce (optional)

✓ *Grocery List*
  PITA BREAD ROUNDS
  COOKED TURKEY BREAST
  SWISS CHEESE
  BASIL PESTO
  LETTUCE

DIRECTIONS

1. In a medium mixing bowl combine turkey, cheese, celery, and carrot; add mayonnaise and pesto, stirring until combined. Spoon mixture into each pita pocket. If desired, top with lettuce.

SHE REMEMBERED TOO LATE!

A LITTLE PESTO GOES A LONG WAY. I AM HAUNTED BY THOSE WORDS. NEXT TIME I HAVE SOME LEFT OVER, AND PLAN TO USE IT IN A DAY OR TWO, I'LL STORE IT IN A COVERED JAR IN THE REFRIGERATOR WITH A THIN LAYER OF OIL POURED ON TOP. FOR LONGER STORAGE, I CAN SPOON THE PESTO INTO ICE CUBE TRAYS AND FREEZE IT. THEN, I'LL POP OUT THE BLOCKS OF PESTO, PLACE THEM IN A FREEZER BAG, AND STORE THEM IN THE FREEZER FOR UP TO ONE MONTH.

NUTRITION FACTS PER SANDWICH: 629 calories, 36 g total fat (9 g saturated fat), 104 mg cholesterol, 647 mg sodium, 39 g carbohydrates, 0 g fiber, 36 g protein. Daily Values: 32% vit. A, 2% vit. C, 29% calcium, 21% iron.

BEEFY QUESADILLAS

WORD TO THE COOK! SOME APPETIZER-TYPE FOODS CAN BECOME DINNER IF YOU BEEF THEM UP JUST RIGHT. CASE IN POINT: THIS FILLING QUESADILLA.

INGREDIENTS

Makes 4 quesadillas
Prep: 10 min. **Cook:** 3 min. per batch

- 4 6- to 8-inch flour tortillas
- ¼ cup mango chutney, chopped
- 1 tablespoon Dijon-style mustard
- 1 teaspoon curry powder
- 6 ounces thinly sliced cooked roast beef
- 1 cup shredded cheddar cheese (4 ounces)
  Sour cream or plain yogurt (optional)

✓ *Grocery List*
ROAST BEEF
CHEDDAR CHEESE
SOUR CREAM (OR PLAIN YOGURT)

DIRECTIONS

1. To soften tortillas, wrap in foil; heat in a 350° oven for 10 minutes. Meanwhile, in a bowl combine the chutney, mustard, and curry powder.
2. Spread chutney mixture over half of each tortilla, leaving a ½-inch border around the edge. Top each with roast beef and cheese. Fold tortillas in half, pressing gently.
3. In a large skillet cook the tortillas over medium to medium-low heat about 3 minutes or until lightly browned, turning once. If desired, serve with sour cream.

HAM AND CHEESE QUESADILLA: Prepare as above, except omit the curry powder. Substitute thinly sliced cooked ham for the roast beef and shredded Swiss cheese for the cheddar.

NUTRITION FACTS PER QUESADILLA: 368 calories, 17 g total fat (8 g saturated fat), 68 mg cholesterol, 469 mg sodium, 30 g carbohydrate, 1 g fiber, 23 g protein. Daily Values: 10% vit. A, 1% vit. C, 21% calcium, 19% iron.

HOT CORNED BEEF & Slaw

DOWN SOUTH THEY'RE APT TO SLAP SOME SLAW ON PULLED PORK TO ADD TANG. THIS RECIPE APPLIES THE CONCEPT TO HOT CORNED BEEF.

INGREDIENTS

Makes 4 sandwiches
Prep: 12 min. **Cook:** 6 min.

- 8   thick slices rye bread
- 2   tablespoons mustard (such as prepared, spicy brown, honey, or Dijon-style)
- 12 ounces thinly sliced cooked corned beef
- ¾   cup deli coleslaw, drained
- 4   slices Swiss cheese (4 ounces)
- 4   teaspoons butter or margarine

✓ *Grocery List*
   RYE BREAD
   CORNED BEEF
   COLESLAW
   SWISS CHEESE

DIRECTIONS

1. Spread 4 of the bread slices with mustard; top with corned beef, coleslaw, and cheese. Top with remaining slices of bread. Melt butter over medium-low heat on a griddle or in a very large skillet. Add sandwiches; cook 3 to 4 minutes per side or until bread is toasted and sandwich is heated through. Great served with chips or deli potato salad and accompanied with a dill pickle.

NUTRITION FACTS PER SANDWICH: 563 calories, 32 g total fat (13 g saturated fat), 121 mg cholesterol, 1,711 mg sodium, 37 g carbohydrate, 0 g fiber, 30 g protein. Daily Values: 11% vit. A, 23% vit. C, 28% calcium, 29% iron.

the Ultimate SLOPPY JOE

FETA, BULGUR, AND A LITTLE OREGANO MAKE THESE JOES MORE THAN THE USUAL KIDS' STUFF. ADD LAMB, AND THEY'RE DOWNRIGHT COSMOPOLITAN.

INGREDIENTS

Makes 6 sandwiches
Prep: 15 min. **Cook:** 10 min.

- 1 pound lean ground lamb or beef
- ½ cup chopped onion
- 1 15-ounce can tomato sauce
- ⅓ cup bulgur
- 1 teaspoon dried oregano, crushed
- 2 cups chopped romaine
- 6 kaiser rolls, split and toasted
- 2 ounces crumbled tomato and basil feta cheese or plain feta cheese

✓ *Grocery List*
GROUND LAMB OR BEEF
ROMAINE
KAISER ROLLS
FETA CHEESE

DIRECTIONS

1. In a 10-inch skillet cook lamb and onion until meat is brown and onion is tender; drain off fat. Stir in tomato sauce, bulgur, and oregano. Bring to boiling. Reduce heat and simmer, uncovered, about 10 minutes or until desired consistency, stirring occasionally.

2. Arrange romaine on bottom halves of rolls. Top with meat mixture. Sprinkle feta cheese over the meat. Cover with top halves of buns.

WHO'S JOE ANYWAY?

EVER WONDER HOW THE SLOPPY JOE GOT ITS NAME? BEATS US! THE SLOPPY PART OF THE NAME IS THE EASY PART, BUT WHO'S JOE? ONE PRETTY RELIABLE SOURCE SAYS THE SANDWICH MIGHT HAVE ORIGINATED IN A SIOUX CITY, IOWA, CAFE, WHERE THE COOK'S NAME WAS (YOU GUESSED IT) JOE. BUT DON'T QUOTE US ON THAT!

NUTRITION FACTS PER SANDWICH: 396 calories, 15 g total fat (6 g saturated fat), 59 mg cholesterol, 889 mg sodium, 43 g carbohydrate, 3 g fiber, 22 g protein. Daily Values: 13% vit. A, 15% vit. C, 11% calcium, 25% iron.

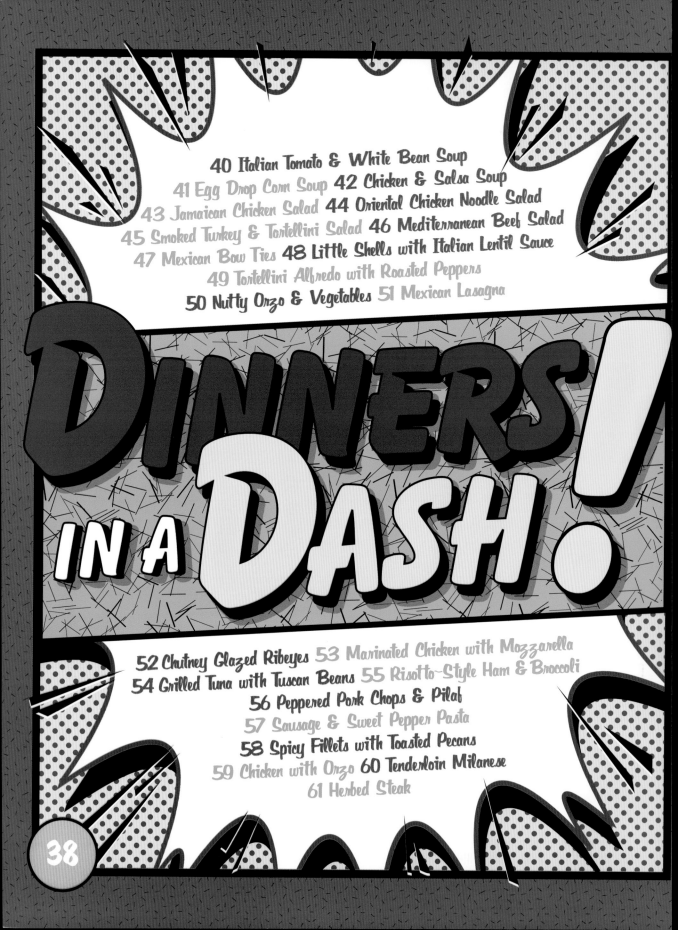

Dinners! In a Dash.

Italian Tomato & White Bean Soup

GO AHEAD! CALL THE WHITE KIDNEY BEANS "CANNELLINI BEANS." THEY'RE THE SAME THING, EXCEPT ONE SOUNDS SEXIER.

INGREDIENTS

Makes 4 servings

Start to finish: 25 min.

- 4 slices bacon
- 1 cup frozen chopped onions
- 1½ teaspoons bottled minced garlic
- 1 28-ounce can crushed tomatoes
- 1 15½-ounce can white kidney beans, rinsed and drained
- 1 14½-ounce can chicken broth
- ⅓ cup snipped fresh basil
- 1 teaspoon sugar
- ¼ cup finely shredded Romano cheese

✓ *Grocery List*
BACON
FRESH BASIL
ROMANO CHEESE

DIRECTIONS

1. In a large saucepan cook bacon until crisp. Remove bacon, reserving 1 tablespoon drippings in pan. Drain bacon on paper towels. Crumble bacon; set aside.

2. Cook onions and garlic in drippings until tender. Add crushed tomatoes, beans, chicken broth, 3 tablespoons of the basil, and sugar. Bring to boiling. Reduce heat and simmer, uncovered, for 10 minutes. Season to taste with pepper.

3. To serve, top each serving with crumbled bacon, Romano cheese, and the remaining basil.

VARIATIONS

CREAM OF TOMATO SOUP: Prepare as above, except omit the bacon. Cook onions and garlic in 1 tablespoon cooking oil. Before serving, stir in ¼ cup whipping cream. Top each serving with remaining basil.

MEXICAN TOMATO SOUP: Prepare as above, except add 1 seeded and finely chopped fresh or bottled jalapeño pepper to the onions and garlic. Omit the basil and Romano cheese. Top each serving with ¼ cup shredded Monterey Jack cheese and 2 tablespoons snipped fresh cilantro.

NUTRITION FACTS PER SERVING: 233 calories, 6 g total fat (2 g saturated fat), 13 mg cholesterol, 1,298 mg sodium, 34 g carbohydrate, 7 g fiber, 16 g protein. Daily Values: 20% vit. A, 23% vit. C, 9% calcium, 17% iron.

EGG DROP CORN SOUP

EAST MEETS MIDWEST IN THIS CORN CHOWDER. IT FEATURES SILKY THREADS OF EGGS—AN IDEA WE SNAGGED FROM ASIAN EGG DROP SOUP.

INGREDIENTS

Makes 6 to 8 servings
Prep: 10 min. **Cook:** 15 min.

- ½ cup finely chopped green onions
- 2 cloves garlic, minced
- 1 tablespoon cooking oil
- 1 49½-ounce can chicken broth
- 1 14¾-ounce can cream-style corn
- ½ teaspoon ground red pepper
- 1 9-ounce package (2 cups) frozen chopped, cooked chicken breast, thawed (optional)
- 2 beaten eggs
- 1 finely chopped green onion

✓ *Pantry only... no shopping required!*

DIRECTIONS

1. In a large saucepan cook onions and garlic in hot oil for 4 to 5 minutes or until onion is tender. Stir in chicken broth, corn, and pepper. Bring to boiling. Reduce heat and simmer, covered, for 5 minutes.

2. If desired, stir in chicken; heat through. Pour the eggs into the soup in a steady stream while stirring 2 or 3 times to create shreds. Top each serving with the additional green onion.

POACH YOUR OWN CHICKEN

THIS RECIPE CALLS FOR FROZEN CHOPPED, COOKED CHICKEN BREAST, WHICH IS ABOUT AS EASY TO USE AS BOLOGNA (EXCEPT YOU HAVE TO THAW IT—IN THE REFRIGERATOR, REMEMBER). BUT IF YOU WANT TO COOK YOUR OWN, HERE'S HOW:

IN A LARGE SKILLET, PLACE 12 OUNCES SKINLESS, BONELESS CHICKEN BREASTS AND 1½ CUPS WATER. BRING TO BOILING; REDUCE HEAT. COVER AND SIMMER FOR 12 TO 14 MINUTES OR UNTIL CHICKEN IS TENDER AND NO LONGER PINK. DRAIN WELL. CUT UP THE CHICKEN. THIS WILL YIELD ABOUT 2 CUPS.

NUTRITION FACTS PER SERVING: 136 calories, 6 g total fat (1 g saturated fat), 72 mg cholesterol, 964 mg sodium, 14 g carbohydrate, 1 g fiber, 8 g protein. Daily Values: 6% vit. A, 9% vit. C, 1% calcium, 7% iron.

CHICKEN & SALSA SOUP

TORTILLA CHIPS DO MORE THAN DIP—HERE, THEY FLOAT, AND GET ALONG SWIMMINGLY WITH THE COLORFUL INGREDIENTS IN THIS MAIN-DISH SOUP.

INGREDIENTS

Makes 4 servings

Prep: 10 min. **Cook:** 13 min.

- 1¾ cups water
- 1 14½-ounce can reduced-sodium chicken broth
- ½ pound skinless, boneless chicken, cut into bite-size pieces
- 1 to 2 teaspoons chili powder
- 1 11-ounce can whole kernel corn with sweet peppers, drained
- 1 cup chunky garden-style salsa
- 3 cups broken, baked, or fried corn tortilla chips
- ½ cup shredded Monterey Jack cheese with jalapeño peppers (2 ounces)

✓ Grocery List

MONTEREY JACK CHEESE WITH JALAPEÑO PEPPERS

DIRECTIONS

1. In a 3-quart saucepan combine water, chicken broth, chicken, and chili powder. Bring to boiling. Reduce heat; simmer, covered, 8 minutes. Add corn. Simmer, uncovered, for 5 minutes more. Stir in salsa; heat through.

2. To serve, top each serving with chips and cheese.

SUDDENLY IT ALL MADE SENSE...

FOR A SIDE DISH, I'LL DISGUISE A 15-OUNCE PACKAGE OF CORNBREAD MIX AS SOMETHING SPECIAL. I'LL JUST STIR IN A DRAINED, 4-OUNCE CAN OF DICED GREEN CHILES BEFORE SPREADING THE BATTER IN THE PAN! THEN I'LL SPRINKLE PAPRIKA ON TOP AND BAKE AS IT SAYS TO ON THE PACKAGE.

NUTRITION FACTS PER SERVING: 319 calories, 9g total fat (3 g saturated fat), 42 mg cholesterol, 989 mg sodium, 32 g carbohydrate, 3 g fiber, 20g protein. Daily Values: 16% vit. A, 43% vit. C, 10% calcium.

JAMAICAN CHICKEN SALAD

THE JERK-SPICED CHICKEN WILL BE JAMAICAN YOU CRAZY FOR THIS BOLD-TASTING SALAD. BUY READY-MADE SEASONING, OR MAKE YOUR OWN.

INGREDIENTS

Makes 4 servings
Start to finish: 25 min.

- ½ cup bottled fat-free honey-Dijon salad dressing
- 1 teaspoon finely shredded lime peel
- 4 skinless, boneless chicken breast halves (1 pound)
- 2 to 3 teaspoons Jamaican Jerk Seasoning
- 2 teaspoons cooking oil
- 1 16-ounce package (12 cups) torn mixed salad greens
- 16 refrigerated mango slices in light syrup, drained, or 2 large fresh mangoes, peeled, seeded, and sliced

✓ Grocery List
  LIMES
  MANGO
  FRESH GREENS

DIRECTIONS

1. For dressing, stir together salad dressing and lime peel. If necessary, add water to make of drizzling consistency. Cover and chill dressing until ready to serve.

2. Rinse chicken; pat dry. Sprinkle chicken with Jamaican Jerk Seasoning. In a large skillet cook the seasoned chicken in hot oil over medium-high heat about 6 minutes per side or until golden brown and no longer pink. Thinly bias-slice each chicken breast.

3. Divide salad greens among 4 dinner plates. Arrange warm chicken and mangoes on top of greens; drizzle with dressing. If desired, top with strips of lime peel.

JAMAICAN JERK SEASONING: Combine 2 teaspoons onion powder, 1 teaspoon sugar, 1 teaspoon crushed red pepper, 1 teaspoon crushed dried thyme, ½ teaspoon salt, ½ teaspoon ground cloves, ½ teaspoon ground cinnamon. Store in a covered container.

NUTRITION FACTS PER SERVING: 318 calories, 6 g total fat (1 g saturated fat), 45 mg cholesterol, 572 mg sodium, 35 g carbohydrate, 8 g fiber, 22 g protein. Daily Values: 153% vit. A, 127% vit. C, 4% calcium, 37% iron.

43

ORIENTAL CHICKEN NOODLE SALAD

STILL HAVEN'T SHAKEN YOUR COLLEGIATE PENCHANT FOR RAMEN NOODLES? TRY THEM IN THIS COLORFUL SALAD. NO HOT POT NEEDED.

INGREDIENTS

Makes 4 servings

Start to finish: 20 min.

- 1   3-ounce package chicken-flavored ramen noodles
- 1   cup fresh pea pods or ½ of a 6-ounce package frozen pea pods, thawed
- 1½ cups frozen chopped, cooked chicken breast, thawed
- 1½ cups shredded Chinese cabbage or cabbage
- 1   8¾-ounce can whole baby corn, drained and halved
- ¼   cup bottled Italian salad dressing
- 1   tablespoon soy sauce
- 1   tablespoon toasted sesame seed

✓ *Grocery List*
PEA PODS
CHINESE CABBAGE

DIRECTIONS

1. Reserve flavoring packet from noodles for another use. Cook noodles according to package directions; drain. Rinse with cold water; drain again.

2. Meanwhile, if using fresh pea pods, trim ends and remove strings. In a large salad bowl combine pea pods, chicken, cabbage, corn, and cooked noodles.

3. For dressing, in a screw-top jar combine salad dressing, soy sauce, and sesame seed. Cover and shake well. Pour over salad; toss to coat.

NUTRITION FACTS PER SERVING: 235 calories, 13 g total fat (2 g saturated fat), 54 mg cholesterol, 507 mg sodium, 9 g carbohydrate, 2 g fiber, 19 g protein. Daily Values: 7% vit. A, 49% vit. C, 4% calcium, 12% iron.

SMOKED TURKEY & TORTELLINI SALAD

TODAY, SUPERMARKETS BRIM WITH CONVENIENCE FOODS (LIKE TORTELLINI) THAT AUNT ALICE AND UNCLE CHARLIE COULD ONLY DREAM OF.

INGREDIENTS

Makes 4 servings

Start to finish: 25 min.

- 1 8-ounce package dried cheese-filled tortellini
- 1 cup chopped cooked smoked turkey, ham, or chicken
- 8 cherry tomatoes, halved
- ½ cup coarsely chopped green sweet pepper
- ¼ cup sliced pitted ripe olives
- ¼ cup bottled balsamic vinaigrette salad dressing

✓ *Grocery List*

SMOKED TURKEY, HAM OR CHICKEN

DIRECTIONS

1. Cook tortellini according to package directions; drain. Rinse with cold water; drain again. In a medium mixing bowl combine tortellini, smoked turkey, tomatoes, sweet pepper, and olives. Drizzle salad dressing over mixture; toss to coat. Season to taste with pepper.

Serve immediately.

OPTION: If your family prefers veggies to meat, replace the ham with 1 cup chopped raw broccoli or cauliflower.

TIME. . . IS ON YOUR SIDE!

YOU SAY YOU WANT TO MAKE THE SALAD A DAY AHEAD AND THEN CHILL IT? NO PROBLEM—BUT FOR THE BEST CONSISTENCY, TOSS THE SALAD WITH AN ADDITIONAL SPLASH OF BALSAMIC VINAIGRETTE DRESSING JUST BEFORE SERVING.

NUTRITION FACTS PER SERVING: 342 calories, 13 g total fat (1 g saturated fat), 20 mg cholesterol, 1,098 mg sodium, 37 g carbohydrate, 1 g fiber, 19 g protein. Daily Values: 3% vit. A, 50% vit. C, 16% calcium, 7% iron.

MEDITERRANEAN BEEF SALAD

BOOK A TRIP TO SHORTCUT CITY: NEXT TIME YOU GRILL, THROW ON AN EXTRA STEAK. THE NEXT DAY, USE IT TO MAKE THIS BEEFY SALAD FAST.

INGREDIENTS

Makes 4 to 6 servings
Prep: 10 min. **Cook:** 14 min.

- 1½ teaspoons dried oregano, crushed
- 1 teaspoon garlic pepper
- ½ cup bottled red wine vinegar-and-oil salad dressing
- 1½ pounds boneless beef top sirloin steak, cut 1 inch thick
- 1 10-ounce package (8 to 9 cups) torn romaine
- ½ of a medium red onion, thinly sliced
- ¼ cup crumbled garlic and herb feta cheese

✓ *Grocery List*

**BEEF TOP SIRLOIN STEAK
ROMAINE
GARLIC AND HERB-FLAVORED
 FETA CHEESE**

DIRECTIONS

1. Combine oregano and garlic pepper; stir ½ teaspoon of the mixture into the dressing. Set aside. Rub remaining mixture evenly onto both sides of steak.

2. Grill steak on the rack of an uncovered grill directly over medium coals to desired doneness, turning once halfway through. (Allow 8 to 12 minutes for medium-rare and 12 to 15 minutes for medium.)

3. Meanwhile, toss together romaine, onion, and feta cheese. Divide romaine mixture among 4 to 6 plates. Thinly slice steak across the grain; arrange steak slices on romaine mixture. Drizzle with some of the salad dressing. Any remaining dressing may be passed at table. Serve with crusty bread.

NUTRITION FACTS PER SERVING: 480 calories, 33 g total fat (9 g saturated fat), 120 mg cholesterol, 589 mg sodium, 6 g carbohydrate, 1 g fiber, 41 g protein. Daily Values: 20% vit. A, 30% vit. C, 6% calcium, 35% iron.

MEXICAN BOW TIES

BOW TIES ARE A GOOD CHOICE FOR THIS DISH. THE SAUCE GETS STUCK IN THE PASTA'S LITTLE FOLDS, MAKING EACH FULL OF FEISTY FLAVORS.

INGREDIENTS

Makes 4 servings
Prep: 5 min. **Cook:** 13 min.

- 8 ounces packaged dried bow ties or medium shell macaroni
- 1 15-ounce can black beans, rinsed and drained
- ¾ cup frozen peas
- ¾ cup shredded cheddar cheese (3 ounces)
- 2 tablespoons butter or margarine, softened
- ½ cup salsa
- ¼ cup dairy sour cream
- 2 tablespoons snipped fresh cilantro

✓ Grocery List
CHEDDAR CHEESE
SOUR CREAM
FRESH CILANTRO

DIRECTIONS

1. Cook pasta according to package directions, adding the beans and peas during the last 1 to 2 minutes of cooking. Drain well; return to pan.
2. Toss pasta mixture with the cheese and butter until melted. Add salsa; toss to coat. Serve immediately topped with sour cream and cilantro.

LET'S GET FRESH!

FEW INGREDIENTS CAN BRING A FRESH FLAVOR TO FOODS SO EASILY AND QUICKLY AS **FRESH HERBS.** TO USE, RINSE THEM FIRST. BUT BE SURE TO **PAT THEM DRY**, BECAUSE IF YOU DON'T THEY'LL CLING TO YOUR KNIFE AS YOU CHOP THEM AND GATHER IN CLUMPS, MAKING IT HARD TO SPRINKLE THEM OVER FOODS. IF YOU'VE GOT KITCHEN SHEARS, EVEN BETTER. PLACE THE HERBS IN A SMALL GLASS MEASURING CUP AND SNIP AWAY— RIGHT IN THE CUP.

NUTRITION FACTS PER SERVING: 459 calories, 19 g total fat (10 g saturated fat), 93 mg cholesterol, 602 mg sodium, 57 g carbohydrate, 8 g fiber, 21 g protein. Daily Values: 21% vit. A, 19% vit. C, 19% calcium, 28% iron.

47

LITTLE SHELLS
with Italian Lentil Sauce

NO DISGUISE NEEDED! HERE A TIMESAVING CAN OF LENTIL SOUP HIDES OUT AS A FRESH AND HEARTY PASTA SAUCE.

INGREDIENTS

Makes 3 or 4 servings
Start to finish: 20 min.

- 1 8-ounce package dried small shell macaroni
- 4 garlic cloves, minced
- 2 tablespoons olive oil
- 1 19-ounce can ready-to-serve lentil soup
- 1 tablespoon lemon juice
- 1 cup halved cherry tomatoes
- ¼ cup finely shredded or grated Romano, Parmesan, or Asiago cheese
- 2 tablespoons snipped fresh parsley

✓ *Grocery List*

LENTIL SOUP
CHERRY TOMATOES
FRESH PARSLEY
ROMANO, PARMESAN, OR
  ASIAGO CHEESE

DIRECTIONS

*1.*Cook pasta according to package directions. Drain well; transfer to a serving dish. Meanwhile, for sauce, in a saucepan cook garlic in hot oil over medium heat about 30 seconds. Add lentil soup and lemon juice; heat through.

*2.*Pour sauce over pasta; add tomatoes. Toss gently to coat. Sprinkle with cheese and parsley.

NUTRITION FACTS PER SERVING: 530 calories, 14 g total fat (3 g saturated fat), 13 mg cholesterol, 671 mg sodium, 81 g carbohydrate, 8 g fiber, 20 g protein. Daily Values: 54% vit. A, 38% vit. C, 13% calcium, 37% iron.

TORTELLINI ALFREDO
with Roasted Peppers

RICH, BOLD, FILLING, COLORFUL, QUICK, DELICIOUS—THERE ARE MORE WORDS TO DESCRIBE THIS DISH THAN INGREDIENTS NEEDED TO MAKE IT!

INGREDIENTS

Makes 3 servings
Start to finish: 20 min.

- 1   9-ounce package refrigerated meat- or cheese-filled tortellini
- 1   4-ounce jar roasted red sweet peppers
- ½   cup refrigerated light alfredo sauce
- ½   cup shredded fresh basil
- ¼   to ½ teaspoon coarsely ground pepper

✓ *Grocery List*
REFRIGERATED TORTELLINI
REFRIGERATED ALFREDO SAUCE
FRESH BASIL

DIRECTIONS

1. Cook tortellini according to package directions; drain. Meanwhile, drain sweet peppers; cut into ½-inch-wide strips.

2. In a large saucepan heat alfredo sauce and add cooked and drained tortellini.

Reduce heat and add sweet peppers; simmer for 5 minutes, stirring often. Stir in half of the basil. Just before serving, top with remaining basil and pepper.

HE MIGHT NEVER HAVE KNOWN...

REFRIGERATED PASTA HAS A SHORT EXPIRATION DATE. BUT CHECK OUT THE PACKAGE TO SEE HOW LONG YOU CAN FREEZE IT. THAT WAY YOU CAN KEEP IT AROUND AWHILE.

NUTRITION FACTS PER SERVING: 362 calories, 12 g total fat (5 g saturated fat), 61 mg cholesterol, 710 mg sodium, 50 g carbohydrate, 1 g fiber, 16 g protein. Daily Values: 19% vit. A, 113% vit. C, 13% calcium, 14% iron.

Dinners in a Dash!

NUTTY ORZO & VEGETABLES

ORZO IS THE PASTA TO USE WHEN YOU ALMOST-BUT-NOT-QUITE FEEL LIKE RICE. HERE IT MELDS WELL WITH A MEDLEY OF COLORFUL, FRESH FLAVORS.

INGREDIENTS

Makes 4 servings

Start to finish: 15 min.

- ½ cup packaged dried orzo (rosamarina)
- 2 cups loose-pack frozen mixed vegetables
- 1 15-ounce can chickpeas (garbanzo beans), rinsed and drained
- 1 14½-ounce can low-sodium stewed tomatoes
- 1¼ cups light spaghetti sauce
- 1 tablespoon snipped fresh thyme
- ¼ cup chopped cashews or slivered almonds, toasted
- ¼ cup shredded reduced-fat mozzarella cheese (1 ounce)

  Fresh thyme (optional)

✓ *Grocery List*

FRESH THYME
MOZZARELLA CHEESE

DIRECTIONS

1. In a large saucepan cook orzo according to package directions, except omit salt; add mixed vegetables after

5 minutes. Drain orzo and vegetables; return to pan. Add chickpeas, undrained tomatoes, spaghetti sauce, and snipped thyme. Bring to boiling. Reduce heat and simmer, covered, for 5 minutes.

2. Stir in cashews or almonds. Divide pasta mixture among 4 dinner plates or bowls. Sprinkle each serving with mozzarella cheese. If desired, garnish with additional thyme.

SUNK!!! UNTIL SHE RECALLED...

SOMETIMES ORZO IS HARD TO FIND IN THE GROCERY STORE. I'LL CHECK THE PASTA AISLE CAREFULLY—TINY, RICE-SHAPED ORZO MAY BE LABELED ROSAMARINA.

50

NUTRITION FACTS PER SERVING: 313 calories, 7 g total fat (2 g saturated fat), 4 mg cholesterol, 364 mg sodium, 53 g carbohydrate, 7 g fiber, 13 g protein. Daily Values: 41% vit. A, 35% vit. C, 7% calcium, 29% iron.

MEXICAN LASAGNA? DON'T WORRY, THE AUTHENTICITY POLICE WON'T COME KNOCKING. FUSING CUISINES IS DELICIOUS—AND DEFINITELY P.C.!

INGREDIENTS

Makes 6 servings
Prep: 10 min. Bake: 30 min.

- 1¼ cups salsa
- 1 15½-ounce can Mexican-style chili beans
- 1 9-ounce package (2 cups) frozen chopped, cooked chicken breast, thawed
- 1 teaspoon chili powder
- ¼ teaspoon ground cumin
- 3 9-inch flour tortillas
- ¾ cup dairy sour cream
- 1½ cups shredded Monterey Jack cheese

Shredded lettuce (optional)
Sliced pitted ripe olives (optional)

✓ Grocery List
SOUR CREAM
MONTEREY JACK CHEESE
LETTUCE

DIRECTIONS

1. Spread ¼ cup of the salsa in the bottom of a 2-quart rectangular baking dish; set aside. Combine remaining salsa, beans, chicken, chili powder, and cumin.

2. To assemble, place one tortilla on top of the salsa, trimming to fit. Top with one-third of the sour cream, one-third of the chicken mixture, and one-third of the cheese. Repeat layers two times, except last layer of cheese.

3. Bake, covered, in a 350° oven for 20 minutes. Top with remaining cheese and bake, uncovered, for 10 to 15 more minutes or until cheese is melted and top is bubbly. Let stand 10 minutes before serving. If desired, sprinkle with lettuce and olives.

NUTRITION FACTS PER SERVING: 401 calories, 22 g total fat (10 g saturated fat), 76 mg cholesterol, 1,054 mg sodium, 29 g carbohydrate, 3 g fiber, 25 g protein. Daily Values: 39% vit. A, 26% vit. C, 26% calcium, 19% iron.

51

CHUTNEY GLAZED RIBEYES

MANGO CHUTNEY IS AS EASY TO USE AS BARBECUE SAUCE, BUT MAKES YOU LOOK TONS MORE EXOTIC! MIX THE GLAZE WHILE THE COALS HEAT.

INGREDIENTS

Makes 4 servings
Prep: 1 min. **Cook:** 15 min.

- ½ cup mango chutney, chopped
- 2 tablespoons Dijon-style mustard
- 2 tablespoons balsamic vinegar
- 1 tablespoon water
- ½ to 1 teaspoon curry powder
- 2 red or yellow sweet peppers, quartered lengthwise
- 1 large sweet onion, cut into ½-inch-thick slices
- 1 tablespoon olive oil or cooking oil
  Salt and pepper
- 4 beef ribeye steaks, cut 1 inch thick (1½ to 2 pounds total)

✓ *Grocery List*
**YELLOW OR RED SWEET PEPPERS
SWEET ONION
BEEF RIBEYE STEAKS**

DIRECTIONS

1. For glaze, stir together the chutney, mustard, balsamic vinegar, water, and curry powder. Set aside.

2. Brush sweet peppers and onion slices with oil; sprinkle with salt. Sprinkle steaks with salt and pepper.

3. Grill steaks and vegetables on the rack of an uncovered grill directly over medium coals until steaks are cooked to desired doneness and vegetables are tender, turning once halfway through. (Allow 8 to 12 minutes for medium-rare and 12 to 15 minutes for medium.) Brush steaks and vegetables with glaze during last 5 minutes of grilling.

Serve steak with peppers* and onions.

*If desired, wrap peppers in foil or a clean paper bag and let stand 10 minutes. Peel skin from peppers.

NUTRITION FACTS PER SERVING: 440 calories, 21 g total fat (8 g saturated fat), 100 mg cholesterol, 358 mg sodium, 26 g carbohydrate, 2 g fiber, 35 g protein. Daily Values: 29% vit. A, 110% vit. C, 2% calcium, 26% iron.

MARINATED CHICKEN
with Mozzarella

THIS ONE'S A BEAUT! WITH RED (FROM THE TOMATOES), WHITE (FROM CHEESE), AND GREEN (BROCCOLI) IT'S LIKE POULTRY IN MOTION!

INGREDIENTS

Makes 4 servings
Start to finish: 20 min.

- 1   6-ounce package long grain and wild rice pilaf mix
- ¼   cup thinly sliced green onions
- ½   cup water
- 1   cup broccoli florets
- 4   marinated skinless, boneless chicken breast halves (about 1 pound total)
- 2   teaspoons olive oil
- 1   medium tomato, halved and thinly sliced
- 2   slices part-skim mozzarella cheese, halved (3 ounces)

✓ Grocery List
BROCCOLI
MOZZARELLA CHEESE

DIRECTIONS

1. Prepare rice pilaf according to package directions, adding green onions the last 5 minutes of cooking.

2. Meanwhile, in a saucepan bring the ½ cup water to boiling; add broccoli. Cook, covered, for 3 minutes or until crisp-tender; drain and set aside.

3. In a large cast-iron skillet cook chicken breasts in hot oil over medium heat for 8 to 10 minutes or until tender and no longer pink, turning once. Overlap the halved tomato slices on top of the chicken breasts. Spoon cooked broccoli on top of tomato slices; cover each with a half-slice of mozzarella.

4. Broil the chicken breasts 3 to 4 inches from the heat about 1 minute or until cheese is melted and bubbly. Serve on hot rice pilaf.

EMERGENCY SUBSTITUTION!

IF PACKAGED, MARINATED CHICKEN BREASTS AREN'T AVAILABLE, USE FRESH BONELESS CHICKEN BREASTS. PAT DRY AND COMBINE WITH ITALIAN SALAD DRESSING, HERB VINAIGRETTE, OR A BOTTLED MARINADE. MARINATE IN THE REFRIGERATOR FOR 4 TO 8 HOURS.

NUTRITION FACTS PER SERVING: 377 calories, 12 g total fat (4 g saturated fat), 22 mg cholesterol, 1,532 mg sodium, 38 g carbohydrate, 2 g fiber, 31 g protein. Daily Values: 14% vit. A, 60% vit. C, 16% calcium, 8% iron.

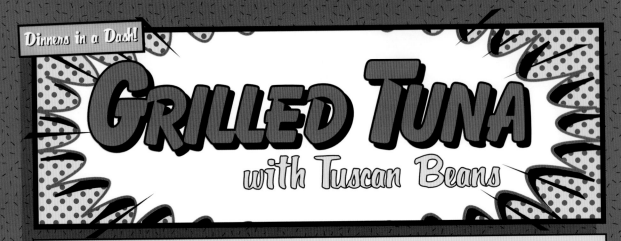

GRILLED TUNA
with Tuscan Beans

JUST A SQUIRT OF LEMON JUICE WILL SPARK THESE TUNA STEAKS, WHILE A CAN OF WHITE BEANS WILL HELP GET THAT TUSCAN THING GOING.

INGREDIENTS

Makes 4 servings
Start to finish: 25 min.

- 1 pound fresh or frozen tuna, swordfish, halibut, shark, or salmon steaks, ½ to 1 inch thick
- 2 cloves garlic, minced
- 1 tablespoon olive oil
- 1 14½-ounce can Italian-style stewed tomatoes, cut up
- 2 teaspoons snipped fresh sage or ¼ teaspoon ground sage
- 1 15-ounce can small white beans, rinsed and drained
- 2 teaspoons olive oil
- 2 teaspoons lemon juice
- ⅛ teaspoon pepper
  Nonstick spray coating
  Fresh sage (optional)

✓ *Grocery List*
TUNA (OR OTHER FISH)
FRESH SAGE

DIRECTIONS

1. Thaw fish, if frozen. For grilling, preheat coals to medium-hot while preparing beans and fish.

2. In a medium skillet cook the garlic in the 1 tablespoon hot oil for 15 seconds. Stir in the undrained tomatoes and the sage. Bring to boiling. Reduce heat and simmer, uncovered, for 5 minutes. Stir in beans; heat through.

3. Meanwhile, rinse fish; pat dry with paper towels. Cut fish into 4 serving-size portions. Brush both sides of fish with the 2 teaspoons oil and the lemon juice; sprinkle with the pepper.

4. Spray an unheated grill rack or grill basket with nonstick coating. Place fish steaks on grill rack or in grill basket. Grill on an uncovered grill directly over medium coals until fish flakes easily when tested with a fork, turning once. (Allow 4 to 6 minutes per ½-inch thickness of fish.) Or, to broil fish, place on the greased unheated rack of a broiler pan. Broil 4 inches from the heat for 4 to 6 minutes per ½-inch thickness of fish.

5. To serve, remove the skin from fish. Spoon bean mixture on each serving plate and top with fish. If desired, garnish with additional sage.

NUTRITION FACTS PER SERVING: 298 calories, 7 g total fat (1 g saturated fat), 49 mg cholesterol, 536 mg sodium, 25 g carbohydrate, 5 g fiber, 33 g protein. Daily Values: 80% vit. A, 22% vit. C, 4% calcium, 18% iron.

RISOTTO-STYLE HAM & BROCCOLI

TRUE RISOTTO INVOLVES STIRRING STOCK INTO RICE UNTIL ABOUT THE TIME THE SUN BURNS OUT. HERE, WE SHAVE OFF THE TIME, NOT THE FLAVOR.

INGREDIENTS

Makes 4 servings
Start to finish: 20 min.

- 2½ cups reduced-sodium chicken broth
- 2 cups quick-cooking brown rice
- 1½ cups chopped broccoli florets
- 1 cup cubed cooked ham (5 ounces)
- ½ of a 10-ounce container (about ½ cup) refrigerated light or regular alfredo sauce
- 2 tablespoons oil-packed dried tomatoes, drained and snipped

✓ Grocery List
   BROCCOLI
   HAM
   REFRIGERATED ALFREDO SAUCE

DIRECTIONS

1. In a 2-quart saucepan bring broth to boiling. Stir in rice. Return to boiling. Reduce heat and simmer, covered, about 10 minutes or until liquid is absorbed.

2. Stir in broccoli, ham, alfredo sauce, and dried tomatoes; heat through.

ORGANIZATION = SUCCESS!!!

KEEP A **GROCERY LIST** ON THE REFRIGERATOR AND WRITE DOWN DEPLETED ITEMS **IMMEDIATELY!**

NUTRITION FACTS PER SERVING: 289 calories, 9 g total fat (4 g saturated fat), 34 mg cholesterol, 1,156 mg sodium, 38 g carbohydrate, 3 g fiber, 16 g protein. Daily Values: 9% vit. A, 69% vit. C, 8% calcium, 6% iron.

55

PEPPERED PORK CHOPS & PILAF

NO MERE '50S-STYLE COMFORT FOOD, THESE SKILLET CHOPS GET WITH THE PROGRAM THANKS TO ROASTED PEPPERS—A HAPPENING INGREDIENT.

INGREDIENTS

Makes 4 servings
Start to finish: 30 min.

- 4   boneless pork loin chops, cut ¾ inch thick
- 1   tablespoon herb-pepper seasoning
- 2   tablespoons olive oil
- 2   cups cut-up vegetables from salad bar (such as sweet peppers, carrots, mushrooms, onions, and/or broccoli)
- 1   14½-ounce can chicken broth
- 2   cups quick-cooking brown rice
- ¼   cup chopped roasted red sweet peppers
      Fresh oregano (optional)

✓ *Grocery List*
   PORK LOIN CHOPS
   SALAD-BAR VEGETABLES
   FRESH OREGANO

DIRECTIONS

1. Trim fat from chops. Sprinkle both sides of meat with 2 teaspoons of the herb-pepper seasoning. In a large skillet cook chops in 1 tablespoon of the olive oil for 5 minutes. Turn chops. Cook for 5 to 7 minutes more or until slightly pink in center and juices run clear.

2. If necessary, cut vegetables into bite-size pieces. In a medium saucepan heat the remaining 1 tablespoon olive oil. Add vegetables; cook and stir for 2 minutes. Carefully add broth. Bring to boiling. Stir in rice, sweet peppers, and the remaining 1 teaspoon herb-pepper seasoning. Return to boiling. Simmer, covered, for 5 minutes. Remove from heat; let stand 5 minutes. Serve chops with rice mixture. If desired, sprinkle chops with fresh oregano.

NUTRITION FACTS PER SERVING: 431 calories, 20 g total fat (5 g saturated fat), 77 mg cholesterol, 408 mg sodium, 34 g carbohydrate, 5 g fiber, 31 g protein. Daily Values: 48% vit. A, 99% vit. C, 2% calcium, 16% iron.

Sausage & Sweet Pepper Pasta

ITALIAN SAUSAGE IS YOUR LINK TO A BOLD MEAL MADE FROM JUST FIVE INGREDIENTS (OK—SIX IF YOU'RE A SMARTY-PANTS AND COUNT THE PEPPER).

INGREDIENTS

Makes 4 servings
Start to finish: 20 min.

- 8 ounces packaged dried bow ties
- ¾ pound fresh spicy Italian sausage links
- 2 medium red sweet peppers, cut into ¾-inch pieces
- ½ cup vegetable broth or beef broth
- ¼ teaspoon coarsely ground pepper
- ¼ cup snipped fresh Italian parsley

✓ *Grocery List*
   **FRESH ITALIAN SAUSAGE LINKS
   RED SWEET PEPPERS
   FRESH ITALIAN PARSLEY**

DIRECTIONS

1. Cook pasta according to package directions; drain well. Meanwhile, cut the sausage into 1-inch pieces. In a large skillet cook sausage and sweet peppers over medium-high heat until sausage is brown. Drain off fat.

2. Add the broth and ground pepper. Bring to boiling. Reduce heat and simmer, uncovered, for 5 minutes. Remove from heat. Toss pasta with sausage mixture and Italian parsley.

DIETING GUESTS? NO PROBLEM!
FOR A LOWER-FAT VERSION, I'LL USE ITALIAN-STYLE GROUND TURKEY SAUSAGE!

Dinners in a Dash!

SPICY FILLETS
with Toasted Pecans

CHOOSE A FISH WITH A FIRM, MEATY TEXTURE. DON'T OVER-TOAST THE PECANS. THAT'S ALL WE'RE TELLING YOU. THAT'S ALL YOU NEED TO KNOW.

INGREDIENTS

Makes 4 servings
Prep: 10 min. **Cook:** 7 min.

- ¼ cup all-purpose flour
- 2 tablespoons yellow cornmeal
- 1 teaspoon chili powder
- ½ teaspoon garlic salt
- 1 pound fresh firm-textured fish fillets, ½ to 1 inch thick (such as catfish, pike, lake trout, or orange roughy)
- 3 tablespoons butter or margarine
- ¼ cup broken pecans
- 1 tablespoon lemon juice
- ⅛ teaspoon ground red pepper (optional)

✓ *Grocery List*
   FRESH FISH

DIRECTIONS

1. In a shallow dish stir together flour, cornmeal, chili powder, and garlic salt. Dip fish into the flour mixture.

2. In a 12-inch skillet cook fish in 2 tablespoons of the butter over medium heat for 4 to 6 minutes per ½-inch thickness or until fish flakes easily and coating is golden, turning once. Remove fish from skillet; keep warm.

3. Melt the remaining 1 tablespoon butter in the skillet; add pecans. Cook and stir over medium heat for 3 to 5 minutes or until lightly toasted. Stir in lemon juice and, if desired, pepper. Drizzle pecan mixture over fish fillets.

NOTHING *FISHY* HERE!

CHOOSE FRESH FISH THAT HAS A MILD SMELL, NOT A STRONG ODOR. WHEN BUYING WHOLE FISH, LOOK FOR CLEAR, BRIGHT EYES, NOT SUNKEN. SELECT FISH WITH BRIGHT RED OR PINK GILLS. CHECK THAT THE SKIN IS SHINY AND ELASTIC, WITH SCALES TIGHTLY IN PLACE. WHEN CHOOSING FRESH FILLETS AND STEAKS, SELECT THOSE THAT APPEAR MOIST AND FRESHLY CUT.

NUTRITION FACTS PER SERVING: 267 calories, 14 g total fat (2 g saturated fat), 45 mg cholesterol, 407 mg sodium, 11 g carbohydrate, 1 g fiber, 24 g protein. Daily Values: 15% vit. A, 9% vit. C, 6% calcium, 9% iron.

CHICKEN WITH ORZO

ENTERTAINING A GREEK TYCOON? NO? WELL TRY THIS GREEK-STYLE DISH ANYWAY. IT'S EXTRA QUICK, THANKS TO A ROTISSERIE CHICKEN SHORTCUT.

INGREDIENTS

Makes 4 to 6 servings
Prep: 25 min. Bake: 10 min.

Nonstick spray coating

1½ cups packaged dried orzo
    (rosamarina) (8 ounces)

2   cups shredded fresh spinach

½   cup crumbled feta cheese
    (2 ounces)

1   teaspoon finely shredded lemon
    peel

1   deli-cooked rotisserie chicken, cut
    into serving-size pieces

1   medium tomato, cut into wedges

✓ Grocery List

FRESH SPINACH
FETA CHEESE
LEMON
ROTISSERIE CHICKEN

DIRECTIONS

1. Spray a 2-quart rectangular baking dish with nonstick coating; set aside.

2. Prepare orzo according to package directions; drain well. Return orzo to saucepan. Add spinach, *half* of the feta cheese, and lemon peel, tossing to combine. Spread orzo mixture in prepared baking dish. Arrange chicken pieces and tomato wedges over orzo mixture. Sprinkle with the remaining feta cheese.

3. Bake, uncovered, in a 450° oven about 10 minutes or until heated through.

ALWAYS A STEP AHEAD...

LEMON PEEL FREEZES WELL. I FREEZE IT IN RESEALABLE PLASTIC BAGS FOR UP TO 3 MONTHS. THAT WAY, IT'S ALWAYS ON HAND.

NUTRITION FACTS PER SERVING: 459 calories, 14 g total fat (6 g saturated fat), 96 mg cholesterol, 446 mg sodium, 48 g carbohydrate, 2 g fiber, 35 g protein. Daily Values: 25% vit. A, 23% vit. C, 17% calcium, 27% iron.

TENDERLOIN MILANESE

TUSCANY MAY BE ITALY'S MOST FAMOUS REGION FOR BEEF, BUT THIS RECIPE PROVES THE MILANESE KNOW THEIR WAY AROUND BEEF, TOO.

INGREDIENTS

Makes 4 servings
Prep: 5 min. **Cook:** 6 min.

- 1 beaten egg
- 2 tablespoons prepared basil pesto
- ½ cup seasoned fine dry bread crumbs
- 3 tablespoons grated Romano or Parmesan cheese
- 4 6-ounce beef tenderloin steaks, cut ½ inch thick
- 2 tablespoons olive oil

✓ *Grocery List*
  PESTO
  ROMANO OR PARMESAN CHEESE
  BEEF TENDERLOIN STEAKS

DIRECTIONS

1. In a shallow dish combine egg and pesto. For coating mixture, in another shallow dish combine bread crumbs and cheese. Dip steaks into egg mixture; coat with crumb mixture.

2. In a 12-inch skillet cook steaks in hot oil uncovered, over medium-high heat (about 6 minutes for medium-rare to medium doneness), turning once (if crumbs brown too quickly, reduce heat to medium). Serve steaks immediately.

NUTRITION FACTS PER SERVING: 436 calories, 25 g total fat (6 g saturated fat), 153 mg cholesterol, 575 mg sodium, 12 g carbohydrate, 0 g fiber, 38 g protein. Daily Values: 3% vit. A, 0% vit. C, 5% calcium, 29% iron.

HERBED STEAK

RICH MEAT. HOT BUTTER. FRESH HERBS. THIS ISN'T YOUR AVERAGE HE-MAN STEAK—IT'S MUCH MORE WORLDLY (BUT JUST AS EASY AND HEARTY).

INGREDIENTS

Makes 4 servings
Prep: 20 min. **Cook:** 8 min.

- 2 beef top loin steaks, cut ¾ inch thick (about 1¼ pounds total)
- 1 tablespoon butter or margarine
- ⅓ cup sliced green onions
- 1½ teaspoons snipped fresh thyme or basil or ½ teaspoon dried thyme or basil, crushed
- ¼ teaspoon salt
- ⅛ teaspoon pepper
- 1 medium tomato, chopped (⅔ cup)

✓ *Grocery List*
  **BEEF TOP LOIN STEAKS
  FRESH THYME OR BASIL**

DIRECTIONS

*1.*Cut each steak in half. In a large, heavy skillet cook steaks in hot butter, uncovered, over medium heat about 10 minutes or to desired doneness, turning once.

*2.*Remove steaks, reserving drippings in skillet; keep steaks warm. Cook green onions, thyme, salt, and pepper in drippings for 1 to 2 minutes or until green onions are tender. Stir in tomato; heat through. Spoon over steaks.

FRESH IS BEST, BUT...

IF YOUR FAVORITE STORE IS OUT OF THE FRESH HERB YOU NEED, AND YOU DON'T FEEL LIKE DRIVING ALL OVER TOWN FOR A MEASLY TABLESPOON OF IT, **YOU CAN SUBSTITUTE** DRIED HERBS. REMEMBER THIS FORMULA: USE ½ TO 1 TEASPOON OF DRIED HERB FOR EACH 1 TABLESPOON SNIPPED FRESH HERB CALLED FOR IN THE RECIPE. CRUSH IT BETWEEN YOUR FINGERS BEFORE YOU ADD IT TO THE RECIPE—THAT HELPS RELEASE SOME OF THE FLAVOR.

NUTRITION FACTS PER SERVING: 207 calories, 9 g total fat (3 g saturated fat), 81 mg cholesterol, 230 mg sodium, 2 g carbohydrate, 0 g fiber, 28 g protein. Daily Values: 7% vit. A, 12% vit. C, 1% calcium, 21% iron.

DING DONG!

Company's Coming!

Patio Party

Greek Salad

Hassleback Potatoes

Lemon-Garlic Pork Chops

Lemon Ice Cream Tart

Greek Salad

A SALAD JUST WOULDN'T BE GREEK WITHOUT FETA AND LOTS OF OLIVES. AND, WHAT THE HECK, WHY NOT GO WILD AND ADD A RADISH, TOO?

INGREDIENTS

Makes 8 servings
Start to finish: 15 min.

- 2 5-ounce bags (12 cups) torn mixed salad greens
- 3 cups chopped, seeded tomatoes (6 medium)
- 1 medium red onion, cut into thin wedges (1 cup)
- 1 cup pitted whole Greek black olives
- 1 cup shredded radishes
- 1 cup crumbled feta cheese (4 ounces)
- ½ to ⅔ cup bottled Italian vinaigrette salad dressing or desired bottled salad dressing

✓ *Grocery List*
MIXED SALAD GREENS
FETA CHEESE
RADISHES

DIRECTIONS

1. In a large salad bowl combine greens, tomatoes, onion, olives, radishes, and cheese. Drizzle salad dressing over mixture, toss to coat.

PLANNING BECAME SECOND NATURE...

SURE I'M BUSY, BUT I'LL JUST MAKE THIS SALAD AHEAD, COVER IT WITH PLASTIC WRAP, AND REFRIGERATE IT UNTIL I'M READY TO SERVE. AND TO KEEP THE SALAD CRISP, I WON'T ADD THE DRESSING UNTIL RIGHT BEFORE SERVING.

NUTRITION FACTS PER SERVING: 160 calories, 13 g total fat (3 g saturated fat), 12 mg cholesterol, 474 mg sodium, 9 g carbohydrate, 2 g fiber, 3 g protein. Daily Values: 85% vit. A, 32% vit. C, 7% calcium, 4% iron.

Hassleback Potatoes

WHO KNOWS WHY THEY'RE CALLED HASSLEBACK POTATOES? THEY SHOULD BE CALLED HASSLE-LESS POTATOES BECAUSE THEY'RE SO EASY!

INGREDIENTS

Makes *8 servings*
Prep: *20 min.* **Cook:** *40 to 50 min.*

- 8 medium baking potatoes, such as russet (6 ounces each)
- ⅓ cup olive oil
- ½ teaspoon pepper
- 1 teaspoon salt

DIRECTIONS

1. Scrub potatoes thoroughly with a brush. Pat dry. Thinly slice potatoes crosswise, but do not cut all the way through. Leave each slice connected to a strip along the bottom of the potato. (Place potatoes in a shallow baking dish or pan. Using your fingers to separate slices, fan potatoes slightly.)

2. In a small bowl combine oil and pepper; drizzle over potatoes. Sprinkle potatoes with salt. Wrap potatoes individually in heavy-duty foil.

3. In a grill with a cover arrange preheated coals around edges of grill. Test for medium heat above center of grill. Place wrapped potatoes in the center of grill, not directly over coals. Cover and grill 40 to 50 minutes or until potatoes are tender. Let stand 10 minutes before serving. Fan potato slices slightly before serving. (Or, bake potatoes in a 400° oven about 40 minutes or until tender.)

NUTRITION FACTS PER SERVING: 256 calories, 9 g total fat (1 g saturated fat), 0 mg cholesterol, 280 mg sodium, 41 g carbohydrate, 1 g fiber, 4 g protein. Daily Values: 0% vit. A, 42% vit. C, 1% calcium, 14% iron.

Lemon-Garlic Pork Chops

AHHH, THE EVER-ACCOMMODATING PORK CHOP! FRESH TARRAGON TEAMS UP WITH LEMON AND GARLIC, MAKING THIS AN ALL-OUT CROWD PLEASER.

INGREDIENTS

Makes 8 servings
Prep: 5 min. **Cook:** 8 min.

- 8 boneless pork loin chops, ¾ inch thick (4 ounces each)
- ¼ cup olive oil
- ¼ cup lemon juice
- 1 tablespoon snipped fresh tarragon or 1 teaspoon dried tarragon, crushed
- 2 teaspoons bottled minced garlic
- 1 teaspoon finely shredded lemon peel
- ½ teaspoon coarsely ground pepper

✓ *Grocery List*
BONELESS LOIN PORK CHOPS
FRESH TARRAGON
LEMON

DIRECTIONS

1. Place chops in a plastic bag set in a shallow dish. For marinade, combine olive oil, lemon juice, tarragon, garlic, lemon peel, and pepper; pour over chops. Close bag. Marinate at room temperature for up to 30 minutes.

2. Remove chops from marinade; reserve marinade. Grill chops on the rack of an uncovered grill directly over medium coals for 8 to 11 minutes, or until still slightly pink in center and juices run clear, turning once and brushing with reserved marinade.

TALK LIKE A CHEF...

NEXT TIME COMPANY COMES, IMPRESS THEM WITH THESE FOODIE TERMS:

MISE EN PLACE: (LITERALLY, "SET IN PLACE") THE INGREDIENTS THAT ARE SET OUT, MEASURED, AND ALL READY TO USE IN A RECIPE. USAGE: "SURE, ROY, I'LL GET YOU A BEER, AS SOON AS I GET MY MISE EN PLACE GOING FOR MY MEAT LOAF." (PRONOUNCED MEEZ-ON-PLASS.)

BATTERIE DE CUISINE: BASICALLY, THIS IS THE SUM OF A KITCHEN'S UTENSILS. USAGE: "CHECK OUT MY BATTERIE DE CUISINE—I'VE GOT A GREAT NEW **SPATULA** YOU REALLY MUST SEE!" (PRONOUNCED BAT-TREE DUH QUEEZEEN.)

NUTRITION FACTS PER SERVING: 157 calories, 10 g total fat (3 g saturated fat), 51 mg cholesterol, 39 mg sodium, 0 g carbohydrate, 0 g fiber, 16 g protein. Daily Values: 0% vit. A, 2% vit. C, 0% calcium, 4% iron.

Lemon Ice Cream Tart

THIS TART IS UTTERLY PAINLESS TO PREPARE, BUT YOUR GUESTS MAY THINK IT WAS THE PRODUCT OF HOURS OF LABOR. LET THEM.

INGREDIENTS

Makes 8 to 10 servings
Prep: 30 min. Freeze: 3 hrs.

- 1 cup graham cracker crumbs
- ½ cup very finely chopped pecans, toasted
- ¼ cup butter or margarine, melted
- 3 tablespoons sugar
- ½ gallon vanilla ice cream, softened
- 2 tablespoons finely shredded lemon peel
- ⅛ teaspoon ground cloves
- ¼ cup lemon juice
- 1 recipe candied lemon slices (optional)

✓ Grocery List
  LEMONS
  VANILLA ICE CREAM

DIRECTIONS

1. For crust, in a medium bowl combine cracker crumbs, pecans, butter, and sugar. Press crumb mixture into the bottom of a 9-inch springform pan. For filling, in a large bowl combine ice cream, lemon peel, lemon juice, and cloves. Spoon filling evenly over crust. Cover with plastic wrap. Freeze for at least 3 hours. If desired, garnish with Candied Lemon Slices.

NOTE: To toast pecans, spread in a shallow baking pan and bake at 350° for 10 to 12 minutes, shaking pan occasionally. (Chop them in a food processor or by hand.)

NOTE: First, allow ice cream to soften in large bowl. Cut it into chunks so it softens more quickly and evenly. Stir occasionally.

CANDIED LEMON SLICES: Combine 1½ cups water and 1 cup sugar in a saucepan. Bring to a boil over medium-high heat, stirring until sugar is dissolved. Add 1 lemon, thinly sliced. Boil gently for 10 minutes. Remove from heat; let lemon slices cool in liquid to room temperature. Remove lemon slices from liquid; drain on cooling rack for 2 to 3 hours or until dried.

NUTRITION FACTS PER SERVING: 428 calories, 26 g total fat (13 g saturated fat), 73 mg cholesterol, 222 mg sodium, 47 g carbohydrate, 1 g fiber, 6 g protein. Daily Values: 20% vit. A, 10% vit. C, 15% calcium, 4% iron.

menu

Salmon Soiree

Sherry-Onion Rice
Green Bean & Blue Cheese Salad
Maple-Hazlenut Salmon
Orange Strawberries

69

Sherry-Onion Rice

USE A GOOD SPANISH SHERRY ALONG WITH THE CHICKEN BROTH AND YOU'LL NEVER THINK OF RICE AS A PLAIN OLD SIDE DISH AGAIN.

INGREDIENTS

Makes 8 to 10 servings
Prep: 10 min. **Cook:** 20 min.

- 2 14½-ounce cans chicken broth
- ⅔ cup dry sherry
- 2 cups uncooked long grain rice
- 2 cups chopped onions
- 1 tablespoon olive oil
- ½ cup chopped pecans, toasted
- ¼ teaspoon freshly ground pepper
- 1 tablespoon snipped fresh oregano

✓ *Grocery List*
FRESH OREGANO
FRESH CHIVES

DIRECTIONS

1. In a large saucepan bring chicken broth and sherry to boiling; stir in rice. Reduce heat and simmer, covered, for 20 minutes or until rice is tender and liquid is absorbed.

2. Meanwhile, in a large skillet, cook onions in hot olive oil over medium heat about 10 minutes or until onions are caramelized (deep golden brown). Stir onions, pecans, and pepper into cooked rice. Sprinkle with oregano.

HE'D STOP AT NOTHING . . .

I'LL DO ANYTHING YOU ASK—JUST NAME IT.

OK, THEN—TOAST THE PECANS FOR ME. SPREAD THEM IN A SHALLOW BAKING PAN AND BAKE THEM AT 350° FOR 10 TO 12 MINUTES. OH, AND DON'T FORGET TO SHAKE THE PAN OCCASIONALLY.

NUTRITION FACTS PER SERVING: 312 calories, 7 g total fat (1 g saturated fat), 0 mg cholesterol, 331 mg sodium, 45 g carbohydrate, 1 g fiber, 6 g protein. Daily Values: 0% vit. A, 2% vit. C, 2% calcium, 17% iron.

Green Bean & Blue Cheese Salad

The key to bringing that nonchalant, "nothing-to-it" aura to a dinner party is to make some dishes ahead. This one's a good choice for that.

INGREDIENTS

Makes *8 servings*
Prep: *10 min.* **Cook:** *10 min.*

- 2 16-ounce packages frozen cut green beans
- 1 cup crumbled blue cheese (4 ounces)
- 1 cup halved and thinly sliced red onion
- ¼ cup olive oil
- 3 tablespoons white wine vinegar or white balsamic vinegar
- 2 teaspoons Dijon-style mustard
- ¼ teaspoon salt
- ¼ teaspoon pepper

✓ *Grocery List*
BLUE CHEESE (NOTE: BLUE CHEESE FREEZES WELL, SO IT CAN BECOME A PANTRY ITEM)

DIRECTIONS

1. Cook beans according to package directions. Place cooked beans in a colander; rinse with cold water until cool. Drain well. In a large salad bowl combine beans, blue cheese, and onion. (If desired, cover and chill for 2 hours.)

2. For dressing, in a screw-top jar combine oil, vinegar, mustard, salt, and pepper. Cover and shake well. (If desired, cover and refrigerate for 2 hours; shake before serving.) To serve, pour dressing over salad; toss to coat.

NUTRITION FACTS PER SERVING: 157 calories, 12 g total fat (4 g saturated fat), 13 mg cholesterol, 349 mg sodium, 9 g carbohydrate, 0 g fiber, 5 g protein. Daily Values: 9% vit. A, 17% vit. C, 12% calcium, 7% iron.

71

Maple-Hazelnut Salmon

CERTAIN TYPES OF FISH, SUCH AS TROUT AND SALMON, SEEM TO INVITE A KISS OF SWEETNESS. MAPLE SYRUP'S THE TICKET HERE.

INGREDIENTS

Makes 8 servings
Prep: 10 min. **Cook:** 8 min.

- 8 6- to 8-ounce salmon fillets, cut about 1 inch thick
   Salt and pepper
- ½ cup pure maple syrup or maple-flavored syrup
- ¾ cup chopped hazelnuts (filberts) or pecans
- 2 tablespoons margarine or butter

✓ *Grocery List*
   SALMON FILLETS

DIRECTIONS

1. Rinse fish; pat dry with paper towels. Arrange fish in a lightly greased 3-quart rectangular baking dish, turning under any thin edges. Sprinkle lightly with salt and pepper. Drizzle maple syrup over fish. Bake, uncovered, in a 450° oven for 8 to 12 minutes or until fish flakes when tested with a fork.

2. Meanwhile, in a medium skillet cook and stir nuts in hot butter over medium heat for 2 to 4 minutes or until lightly toasted. Spoon nut mixture over fillets.

NUTRITION FACTS PER SERVING: 299 calories, 15 g total fat (2 g saturated fat), 31 mg cholesterol, 204 mg sodium, 15 g carbohydrate, 1 g fiber, 26 g protein. Daily Values: 7% vit. A, 0% vit. C, 3% calcium, 2% iron.

Orange Strawberries

YOU COULD CALL THIS LUSCIOUS DISH STRAWBERRIES ROMANOFF—WE DIDN'T BECAUSE WE THOUGHT THAT MIGHT MAKE IT SOUND TOO HARD, AND IT'S NOT!

INGREDIENTS

Makes *8* servings

Prep: 15 min. **Stand:** 30 min.

- 6 cups fresh strawberries, halved
- ¼ cup orange liqueur or ¼ cup orange juice plus ¼ teaspoon almond extract
- ¼ cup granulated sugar
- 2 cups crème fraîche or two 8-ounce cartons vanilla yogurt
- ½ cup brown sugar

✓ *Grocery List*

STRAWBERRIES
CRÈME FRAÎCHE (OR WHIPPING
CREAM AND SOUR CREAM OR
VANILLA YOGURT)

DIRECTIONS

1. In a bowl combine strawberries, orange liqueur, and granulated sugar. Stir gently to coat. Let stand at room temperature for 30 minutes. (Or, cover and refrigerate up to 4 hours, stirring occasionally.) Serve strawberries in small bowls topped with crème fraîche or yogurt. Sprinkle 1 tablespoon brown sugar over each.

YES, SIR! SHE'D GO THE EXTRA MILE!!!

SO WHAT IF THEY DIDN'T HAVE IT AT THE STORE—I'LL MAKE MY OWN CRÈME FRAÎCHE! I CAN STIR TOGETHER ONE CUP OF WHIPPING CREAM (NOT THAT ULTRAPASTEURIZED KIND) WITH ONE 8-OUNCE CARTON OF DAIRY SOUR CREAM, COVER IT, AND LET IT STAND AT ROOM TEMPERATURE FOR TWO TO FIVE HOURS OR UNTIL IT THICKENS SLIGHTLY. THEN IT CAN BE COVERED AND STORED IN THE REFRIGERATOR UNTIL SERVING TIME OR FOR UP TO ONE WEEK.

NUTRITION FACTS PER SERVING: 293 calories, 17 g total fat (11 g saturated fat), 54 mg cholesterol, 33 mg sodium, 32 g carbohydrate, 2 g fiber, 2 g protein. Daily Values: 20% vit. A, 106% vit. C, 6% calcium, 4% iron.

Brunch for a Bunch

Morning Skillet Potatoes

Maple-Mustard Sausages

Baked Cinnamon Bread Custard

Fig Muffins

Morning Skillet Potatoes

LEAVING THE SKINS ON THE POTATOES NOT ONLY SAVES TIME, IT TAPS INTO A DELICIOUS NEW TREND IN RUSTIC, COUNTRY-STYLE COOKING. HOW CONVENIENT!

INGREDIENTS

Makes 10 servings
Prep: 10 min. **Cook:** 15 min.

- 3 tablespoons olive oil
- 2 pounds unpeeled red- or yellow-skinned (such as Yukon gold) potatoes, cut into ½-inch cubes (6 cups)
- 2 cups frozen chopped onions
- ½ teaspoon salt
- ¼ teaspoon ground red pepper

DIRECTIONS

1. Heat oil in a 12-inch nonstick skillet over medium heat. Add potatoes and onions; sprinkle with salt and pepper. Cover and cook for 10 minutes or until potatoes are nearly tender, stirring once or twice. Uncover and cook for 5 minutes more or until potatoes are tender and golden brown, stirring occasionally.

NUTRITION FACTS PER SERVING: 134 calories, 4 g total fat (1 g saturated fat), 0 mg cholesterol, 114 mg sodium, 22 g carbohydrate, 1 g fiber, 2 g protein. Daily Values: 0% vit. A, 21% vit. C, 1% calcium, 10% iron.

Maple-Mustard Sausages

THE MOMENT SYRUP FIRST MEANDERED ACROSS THE PLATE TO SAUSAGE LINKS IS LOST TO HISTORY, BUT BREAKFAST HAS NEVER BEEN THE SAME.

INGREDIENTS

Makes 12 servings
Prep: 5 min. **Cook:** 20 min.

- 2 12-ounce packages (24 links total) frozen link pork sausage, thawed
- ¼ cup packed brown sugar
- ¼ cup pure maple syrup or maple-flavored syrup
- 1½ teaspoons dry mustard

✓ *Grocery List*
   LINK PORK SAUSAGE

DIRECTIONS

1. Cook sausages in a 12-inch skillet according to package directions. Drain fat from skillet. Meanwhile, in a small mixing bowl stir together sugar, syrup, and mustard; add mixture to skillet. Cook, uncovered, over medium heat for 3 to 4 minutes or until sausages are glazed, stirring frequently. Serve immediately.

NUTRITION FACTS PER SERVING: 145 calories, 10 g total fat (3 g saturated fat), 26 mg cholesterol, 399 mg sodium, 8 g carbohydrate, 0 g fiber, 5 g protein. Daily Values: 0% vit. A, 0% vit. C, 1% calcium, 3% iron.

Baked Cinnamon Bread Custard

GET THIS PILLOWY DELIGHT READY FOR THE OVEN THE NIGHT BEFORE SO YOU CAN SPEND MORE QUALITY TIME WITH YOUR OWN PILLOW IN THE MORNING.

INGREDIENTS

Makes 10 servings
Prep: 10 min. **Bake:** 30 min.

- 14 slices firm-textured cinnamon bread, about ½ inch thick
- 6 eggs
- 3 egg yolks
- 1 cup sugar
- 3 cups milk
- 2 cups half-and-half or light cream
- 1 tablespoon vanilla
  Powdered sugar (optional)

✓ *Grocery List*
  CINNAMON BREAD
  HALF-AND-HALF OR LIGHT CREAM

DIRECTIONS

1. Arrange bread in a double layer in a lightly greased 13x9-inch baking pan, cutting bread as necessary to cover bottom of pan.
2. In a large mixing bowl beat together eggs and egg yolks. Beat in sugar. Gradually add milk, half-and-half, and vanilla. Pour egg mixture evenly over bread.
3. Bake in a 375° oven for 25 to 30 minutes or until a knife inserted near center comes out clean. If desired, dust with powdered sugar.

BEAT THE CLOCK!

IF YOU'D LIKE TO MAKE THIS RECIPE AHEAD, PREPARE THE CUSTARD AS ABOVE BUT BEFORE BAKING, COVER AND REFRIGERATE IT FOR SEVERAL HOURS OR OVERNIGHT. BAKE IN A 375° OVEN FOR ABOUT 40 MINUTES.

NUTRITION FACTS PER SERVING: 330 calories, 13 g total fat (6 g saturated fat), 215 mg cholesterol, 262 mg sodium, 42 g carbohydrate, 0 g fiber, 11 g protein. Daily Values: 26% vit. A, 1% vit. C, 16% calcium, 10% iron.

Fig Muffins

NOT FOR ENTERTAINING ONLY! MAKE THESE SWEET, MOIST MUFFINS ANYTIME—IF ANYTHING WILL MAKE YOU LOOK FORWARD TO GETTING UP, THIS IS IT.

INGREDIENTS

Makes 18 muffins
Prep: 15 min. **Bake:** 20 min.

- 2½ cups all-purpose flour
- 1 tablespoon baking powder
- 1½ teaspoons ground cinnamon
- ¼ teaspoon baking soda
- ¼ teaspoon salt
- 1 cup buttermilk
- ⅔ cup packed brown sugar
- ½ cup butter, melted
- 2 eggs, slightly beaten
- ¾ cup chopped dried figs

✓ *Grocery List*
  BUTTERMILK (NOTE: COULD KEEP POWDERED BUTTERMILK AS A PANTRY ITEM)

DIRECTIONS

1. Lightly grease eighteen 2½-inch muffin cups or line with paper bake cups; set aside. In a large mixing bowl combine flour, baking powder, cinnamon, baking soda, and salt. Make a well in the center. In a medium mixing bowl combine buttermilk, brown sugar, butter, and eggs; add all at once to flour mixture. Stir just until moistened. (Batter should be slightly lumpy.) Gently fold in figs.

2. Fill prepared muffin cups about two-thirds full. Bake in a 375° oven for 20 minutes or until golden and a toothpick inserted in center comes out clean. Cool 5 minutes. Remove from pans; serve warm. (Could also bake muffins ahead and reheat in microwave or oven before serving.)

NUTRITION FACTS PER MUFFIN: 160 calories, 6 g total fat (3 g saturated fat), 38 mg cholesterol, 184 mg sodium, 24 g carbohydrate, 1 g fiber, 3 g protein. Daily Values: 6% vit. A, 1% vit. C, 7% calcium, 8% iron.

menu

Fast Fiesta

Mexican Corn & Rice Salad

Spinach & Cheese Tortilla Rolls

Southwestern Salsa Chicken

Quick Mocha Pots de Crème

Mexican Corn & Rice Salad

THIS BRIGHT, LIGHT, AND COLORFUL SALAD IS ALMOST TOO EASY! ALMOST— THERE'S JUST ENOUGH TO IT THAT YOU ARE ALLOWED TO ACCEPT COMPLIMENTS.

INGREDIENTS

Makes 8 to 10 servings
Start to finish: 20 min.

- 3 tablespoons salad oil
- 3 tablespoons lime juice
- 1 11-ounce can white whole kernel corn, drained
- 1 cup cooked long grain rice, chilled
- 1 cup chopped tomato
- ½ cup chopped red onion
- 1 4-ounce can diced green chili peppers, drained
- 2 tablespoons snipped fresh cilantro (optional)

✓ *Grocery List*
FRESH CILANTRO

DIRECTIONS

1. Whisk together oil and lime juice; set aside. In a salad bowl combine corn, rice, tomato, onion, and chili peppers. Pour oil mixture over rice mixture; toss to coat. Serve immediately or cover and chill for several hours or overnight. If desired, stir in cilantro before serving.

MANY A TEAR HAD TO FALL . . .

AT LEAST IT WASN'T ALL IN VAIN—ANY CHOPPED ONION I DON'T USE I CAN PLACE IN A SEALABLE PLASTIC BAG AND FREEZE TO USE LATER.

80

NUTRITION FACTS PER SERVING: 107 calories, 6 g total fat (1 g saturated fat), 0 mg cholesterol, 177 mg sodium, 13 g carbohydrate, 2 g fiber, 2 g protein. Daily Values: 1% vit. A, 22% vit. C,1% calcium, 3% iron.

Spinach & Cheese Tortilla Rolls

YOU'VE PROBABLY SEEN SIMILAR APPETIZERS SERVED COLD. BUT A LITTLE PARMESAN AND A PASS THROUGH THE OVEN MAKE THESE BABIES **HOT!**

INGREDIENTS

Makes 8 to 10 servings
Prep: 10 min. Bake: 10 min.

- 4 8-inch flour tortillas
- 6 ounces tub cream cheese, softened
- ½ cup chopped green onions
- ¼ cup dairy sour cream
- ½ teaspoon garlic salt
- 1 10-ounce package frozen chopped spinach, thawed and well drained
- ¼ cup grated Parmesan cheese

✓ Grocery List
    CREAM CHEESE
    SOUR CREAM
    PARMESAN CHEESE

DIRECTIONS

1. To soften tortillas, wrap in foil; heat in a 350° oven for 10 minutes. Meanwhile, in medium mixing bowl stir together cream cheese, green onions, sour cream, and garlic salt; fold in spinach. Spread a layer of the spinach mixture evenly over one side of each tortilla. Tightly roll up each tortilla. Wrap each roll with plastic wrap and refrigerate for 1 to 4 hours. To serve, cut each roll into ¾-inch-thick slices; place on a cookie sheet cut side down. Sprinkle with Parmesan cheese. Bake in a 400° oven about 10 minutes or until bottoms are lightly browned.

NUTRITION FACTS PER SERVING: 158 calories, 11 g total fat (6 g saturated fat), 28 mg cholesterol, 347 mg sodium, 10 g carbohydrate, 1 g fiber, 5 g protein. Daily Values: 25% vit. A, 6% vit. C, 9% calcium, 6% iron.

Southwestern Salsa Chicken

HOW DID WE EVER LIVE WITHOUT BOTTLED SALSA? AS YOU'LL SEE HERE, IT'S THE ULTIMATE EASY-TO-USE CONDIMENT—A KETCHUP FOR THE NEW MILLENNIUM.

INGREDIENTS

Makes 8 servings

Prep: 5 min. plus 5 min. to assemble

Cook: 8 min.

8   medium skinless, boneless chicken breast halves (about 2 pounds total)

½   cup all-purpose flour

¼   teaspoon salt

¼   teaspoon pepper

3   tablespoons cooking oil or olive oil

1¼   cups salsa

8   6- or 7-inch corn tortillas

3   cups shredded lettuce

½   cup dairy sour cream

¼   cup snipped fresh cilantro

✓ Grocery List

LETTUCE
SOUR CREAM
FRESH CILANTRO

DIRECTIONS

1. Rinse chicken; pat dry. In a plastic bag combine flour, salt, and pepper. Add chicken pieces, a few at a time, shaking to coat. Heat oil in a 12-inch skillet over medium heat; add chicken. Cook, uncovered, 8 to 10 minutes or until chicken is tender and no longer pink, turning once. Drain chicken on paper towels; keep warm.

2. Meanwhile, in a small saucepan heat salsa until bubbly. Wrap tortillas in a microwave-safe paper towel; microcook on 100 percent power (high) for 30 to 60 seconds or until warmed.

3. To serve, divide lettuce among warmed tortillas. Place one chicken breast on each tortilla. Spoon salsa over chicken. Top each with sour cream and cilantro.

NUTRITION FACTS PER SERVING: 295 calories, 13 g total fat (4 g saturated fat), 66 mg cholesterol, 309 mg sodium, 21 g carbohydrate, 0 g fiber, 25 g protein. Daily Values: 9% vit. A, 20% vit. C, 6% calcium, 12% iron.

Quick Mocha Pots de Crème

NO, "POT DE CRÈME" DOESN'T REALLY TRANSLATE AS "ONE HEDONISTIC DESSERT." BUT THESE MOCHA-CREAM TARTS WILL MAKE YOU THINK IT DOES.

INGREDIENTS

Makes 15 tarts

Start to finish: 20 min.

- 1 cup semisweet chocolate pieces
- ¼ cup whipping cream
- 1 tablespoon instant espresso coffee powder or 2 tablespoons instant coffee crystals
- 1 2.1-ounce package (15) baked miniature phyllo dough shells
- ¼ cup whipping cream, whipped

  Instant espresso coffee powder or chocolate curls (optional)

✓ Grocery List
WHIPPING CREAM

DIRECTIONS

1. For filling, in a heavy small saucepan heat and stir chocolate pieces, unwhipped cream, and espresso coffee powder over low heat until smooth. Remove from heat; let stand about 10 minutes until slightly thickened.

2. Spoon filling into phyllo shells. (If desired, cover and chill up to 8 hours. Let stand 15 minutes before serving.) Just before serving, top with whipped cream. If desired, garnish with a sprinkle of espresso coffee powder or chocolate curls.

NUTRITION FACTS PER TART: 104 calories, 7 g total fat (2 g saturated fat), 11 mg cholesterol, 13 mg sodium, 10 g carbohydrate, 0 g fiber, 1 g protein. Daily Values: 3% vit. A, 0% vit. C, 0% calcium, 3% iron.

menu

Saturday Night Sensation

Sun-Dried Tomato Spread

Quick Bread Salad

Glazed Carrot & Parsnip Coins

Chicken Alfredo

Kiwi-Lime Tarts

Sun-Dried Tomato Spread

If you're a sun-dried tomato fan, consider doubling this recipe just to keep it from disappearing even more quickly than it goes together.

INGREDIENTS

Makes 1 cup

Prep: 30 min. Chill: 4 hrs.

- 1 to 2 cloves garlic, minced
- 1 tablespoon olive oil
- ½ cup dried tomatoes (not oil-packed), snipped
- ⅓ cup dry white wine
- 1 8-ounce package cream cheese, softened
- ⅓ cup snipped fresh basil
- 3 tablespoons grated Parmesan cheese

Baguette-style French bread slices, toasted

Fresh basil (optional)

✓ *Grocery List*

CREAM CHEESE
FRESH BASIL
FRENCH BREAD
PARMESAN CHEESE

DIRECTIONS

1. In a medium skillet cook garlic in oil until light brown; add dried tomatoes and wine. Cook, uncovered, over low heat for 15 minutes. Remove from heat; let stand 10 minutes. Drain excess liquid.

2. Meanwhile, in a food processor bowl or blender container combine cream cheese, basil, and Parmesan cheese. Cover and process or blend until smooth. Add tomato mixture; process until almost smooth. Transfer to serving bowl. Cover and chill for 4 to 24 hours. Let stand at room temperature 30 minutes before serving. Serve with toasted baguette slices. If desired, garnish with additional basil.

SERVING SUGGESTIONS? CHILD'S PLAY!

THIS RECIPE WOULD BE GREAT WITH **LOTS** OF OTHER ITALIAN APPETIZERS. **PICK UP SOME IMPORTED ITALIAN OLIVES, CHEESES**– AUTHENTIC, IMPORTED PARMIGIANO-REGGIANO AND TALEGGIO WOULD BE FANTASTIC–AND MAYBE SOME **CURED MEATS, SUCH AS PROSCIUTTO OR ITALIAN SALAMI.**

NUTRITION FACTS PER SERVING: 25 calories, 2 g total fat (1 g saturated fat), 6 mg cholesterol, 36 mg sodium, 1 g carbohydrate, 0 g fiber, 1 g protein. Daily Values: 2% vit. A, 0% vit. C, 1% calcium, 0% iron.

Quick Bread Salad

BREAD SALAD? IF YOU'VE TRIED "PANZANELLA" (A SIMILAR ITALIAN SALAD), YOU MAY ALREADY BE HIP TO THE IDEA. IF NOT, YOU'RE IN FOR A NEW TREAT.

INGREDIENTS

Makes 8 servings

Start to finish: 15 min.

- 6 ounces whole wheat sourdough or other country-style bread, cut into ¾-inch cubes (about 3 cups)
- 8 cups purchased (Italian-style) torn mixed salad greens
- 1 medium tomato, cut into thin wedges
- ½ cup yellow sweet pepper cut into ½-inch pieces
- ½ cup pitted Greek black olives or pitted ripe olives
- ½ cup bottled red wine vinegar and oil salad dressing

✓ *Grocery List*

SOURDOUGH BREAD
MIXED SALAD GREENS
YELLOW SWEET PEPPER

DIRECTIONS

1. Spread bread cubes in a shallow baking pan. Bake in a 375° oven for 10 minutes or until toasted, stirring once. Meanwhile, in a large salad bowl combine salad greens, tomato wedges, sweet pepper, and olives. (If desired, cover and refrigerate for up to 4 hours.) To serve, drizzle dressing over salad mixture; toss to coat. Add bread cubes; toss again. Serve immediately.

NUTRITION FACTS PER SERVING: 154 calories, 10 g total fat (1 g saturated fat), 0 mg cholesterol, 440 mg sodium, 15 g carbohydrate, 1 g fiber, 3 g protein. Daily Values: 2% vit. A, 27% vit. C, 2% calcium, 5% iron.

Glazed Carrot & Parsnip Coins

BROWN SUGAR AWAKENS THE NATURAL SWEETNESS IN THE CARROTS. VINEGAR ADDS JUST ENOUGH TANG TO KEEP YOU FROM CONFUSING THIS WITH DESSERT.

INGREDIENTS

Makes 8 servings
Prep: 10 min. **Cook:** 10 min.

- 1½ pounds medium carrots and/or parsnips, peeled and sliced ¼ inch thick
- ¼ cup packed brown sugar
- 2 tablespoons olive oil
- 2 tablespoons balsamic vinegar or white wine vinegar
- 1 teaspoon cornstarch
  Dash salt
  Pepper

✓ *Grocery List*
  PARSNIPS

DIRECTIONS

1. In a medium saucepan cook carrots, covered, in a small amount of boiling salted water for 7 to 9 minutes or until crisp-tender. Drain carrots; remove from pan.

2. In the same saucepan combine the brown sugar, olive oil, vinegar, cornstarch, and salt. Cook and stir over medium heat until slightly thickened. Add carrots; cook, uncovered, about 2 minutes more or until carrots are glazed, stirring frequently. Season to taste with pepper.

HE WAS FIRM IN HIS CONVICTIONS...

OVER THE TOP, YOU SAY? **NO WAY!** ALPHABETIZING MY SPICES IN SPICE RACKS HELPS ME QUICKLY AND EASILY LOCATE THOSE I NEED, AND MAKES ME LESS LIKELY TO BUY DUPLICATES, SAVING ME TIME AND MONEY!!!

NUTRITION FACTS PER SERVING: 91 calories, 4 g total fat (0 g saturated fat), 0 mg cholesterol, 71 mg sodium, 15 g carbohydrates, 3 g fiber, 1 g protein. Daily Values: 192% vit. A, 4% vit. C, 2% calcium, 5% iron.

87

Chicken Alfredo

A ROMAN RESTAURATEUR INVENTED THE RICH ALFREDO SAUCE. YEARS LATER, SOME CLEVER FOOD MANUFACTURERS MADE IT CONVENIENT. THANK THEM BOTH.

INGREDIENTS

Makes 8 servings

Prep: 15 min. **Bake:** 10 min.

- 8 medium skinless, boneless chicken breast halves (about 2 pounds total)
- ⅛ teaspoon salt
- ⅛ teaspoon pepper
- 2 tablespoons cooking oil
- 1 10-ounce container refrigerated alfredo sauce (about 1 cup)
- 1 7-ounce jar roasted red sweet peppers, drained and cut into strips (1 cup)
- ¼ cup finely shredded fresh basil
- ¼ cup finely shredded Parmesan cheese (1 ounce)

✓ Grocery List

REFRIGERATED ALFREDO SAUCE
FRESH BASIL
PARMESAN CHEESE

DIRECTIONS

1. Rinse chicken; pat dry. Sprinkle with salt and pepper. In a 12-inch skillet cook chicken breasts in hot oil, about 10 minutes, turning to brown evenly. Transfer chicken to a 2-quart rectangular baking dish. Spread alfredo sauce over chicken breasts; top with sweet peppers. Bake, uncovered, in a 350° oven for 10 to 15 minutes or until peppers and sauce are heated through.

2. To serve, sprinkle each chicken breast with basil and Parmesan cheese.

NUTRITION FACTS PER SERVING: 283 calories, 19 g total fat (1 g saturated fat), 80 mg cholesterol, 257 mg sodium, 4 g carbohydrate, 0 g fiber, 25 g protein. Daily Values: 10% vit. A, 85% vit. C, 3% calcium, 6% iron.

Kiwi-Lime Tarts

HOLD IT! DON'T FLIP THE PAGE JUST BECAUSE YOU SEE THE WORD "TART." THIS ONE'S EASY BECAUSE IT STARTS WITH A READY-TO-ROLL COOKIE DOUGH.

INGREDIENTS

Makes 24 tarts
Prep: 20 min. **Cook:** 8 min.

  Nonstick spray coating
- ½ of an 18-ounce roll refrigerated sugar cookie dough
- 1 14-ounce can (1¼ cups) sweetened condensed milk
- ½ cup dairy sour cream
- ½ teaspoon finely shredded lime peel
- ⅓ cup lime juice
- ½ cup whipping cream
- 1 tablespoon sugar
- 2 kiwi fruit

✓ *Grocery List*

REFRIGERATED COOKIE DOUGH
SOUR CREAM
LIME
WHIPPING CREAM
KIWI

DIRECTIONS

1. For tart shells, spray twenty-four 1¾-inch muffin cups with nonstick spray coating; set aside. Slice sugar cookie dough into 6 slices. Cut each slice into quarters. Press one dough quarter into each muffin cup, dipping fingers into flour, if necessary.

2. Bake in a 375° oven about 8 minutes or until golden. Press centers down with the back of a teaspoon. Cool in pan for 5 minutes. Remove from pans; cool completely on a wire rack.

3. Meanwhile, for filling, in a medium mixing bowl combine sweetened condensed milk, sour cream, lime peel, and lime juice; stir until combined. Cover and chill until ready to serve or up to 24 hours.

4. Just before serving, in a chilled bowl beat whipping cream and sugar with the chilled beaters of an electric mixer until soft peaks form; set aside. Peel and halve each kiwi fruit. Cut each half into 6 slices. Spoon filling into tart shells. Top with whipped cream and kiwi fruit.

TO MAKE THIS AHEAD...

ALL THE COMPONENTS OF THIS DESSERT, EXCEPT THE WHIPPED CREAM, CAN BE MADE A DAY AHEAD OF TIME. BUT TO **AVOID SOGGY TART SHELLS**, HOLD OFF ON FILLING THEM UNTIL JUST BEFORE SERVING.

NUTRITION FACTS PER SERVING: 132 calories, 6 g total fat (3 g saturated fat), 16 mg cholesterol, 70 mg sodium, 17 g carbohydrate, 0 g fiber, 2 g protein. Daily Values: 5% vit. A, 14% vit. C, 5% calcium, 1% iron.

DESSERTS IN A FLASH!

CHOCOLATE CHIP ICE CREAM CAKE

THE HOLLOWED-OUT INSIDE OF AN ANGEL FOOD CAKE IS FILLED WITH AN ICE-CREAM/CREAM CHEESE FILLING FOR A TUNNEL YOU'LL LOVE!

INGREDIENTS

Makes 10 to 12 servings
Prep: 20 min. **Freeze:** 3 hrs.

- 1 3-ounce package cream cheese, softened
- 1 tablespoon sugar
- 1½ cups chocolate chip, strawberry, or vanilla ice cream
- 1 8- or 9-inch purchased angel food cake (15 or 16 ounces)
- ⅓ cup sliced strawberries
- ⅓ cup chocolate fudge or strawberry ice cream topping

✓ *Grocery List*
  CREAM CHEESE
  CHOCOLATE CHIP ICE CREAM
  ANGEL FOOD CAKE
  STRAWBERRIES

DIRECTIONS

1. For filling, in a small bowl stir together cream cheese and sugar. In a medium bowl, stir ice cream just until it begins to soften; fold cream cheese mixture into ice cream. Place in freezer while preparing the cake.

2. To hollow out cake, use a serrated knife to cut off the top ½ inch of the cake; set top aside. With the knife held parallel to the side of the cake, cut around the hole in the center of cake, leaving about a ¾-inch thickness of cake around hole. Next, cut around inside the outer edge of the cake, leaving the outer cake wall about ¾ inch thick. Using a spoon, remove center of cake, leaving about a ¾-inch-thick base. (Reserve scooped-out cake for another use.)

3. Spoon filling into hollowed-out section. Arrange the sliced strawberries on top of the filling. Replace the top of the cake. Cover and freeze for several hours, overnight, or until firm.

4. To serve, in a small saucepan heat ice cream topping to drizzling consistency; drizzle over cake. Slice cake with a serrated knife.

NUTRITION FACTS PER SERVING: 219 calories, 7 g total fat (4 g saturated fat), 18 mg cholesterol, 265 mg sodium, 37 g carbohydrate, 0 g fiber, 5 g protein. Daily Values: 6% vit. A, 4% vit. C, 6% calcium, 2% iron.

CHOCOLATE STRAWBERRY TRIFLE

CALLING ON COOKIES INSTEAD CAKE, PUDDING INSTEAD OF CUSTARD SAUCE, THIS ONE BUCKS TRADITION IN FAVOR OF EASE. (IT'S YUMMY, TOO!)

INGREDIENTS

Makes 6 servings

Start to finish: 15 min.

- 1 4-ounce container refrigerated chocolate pudding
- 1 tablespoon crème de cacao or milk
- ½ of an 8-ounce container frozen whipped dessert topping, thawed
- 1½ cups coarsely crumbled shortbread cookies (about half of a 10-ounce package)
- ¼ cup strawberry preserves
- 2 cups sliced strawberries
  Whole strawberries (optional)

✓ *Grocery List*
  FROZEN WHIPPED DESSERT TOPPING
  SHORTBREAD COOKIES
  CHOCOLATE PUDDING
  STRAWBERRIES

DIRECTIONS

1. In a medium mixing bowl stir together chocolate pudding and crème de cacao; fold in *half* of the dessert topping.

2. In a serving bowl layer *half* of the cookies. Spread *half* of the pudding mixture over cookies. Dot with *half* of the preserves. Top with *half* of the sliced strawberries. Repeat layers. Cover and chill up to 4 hours.

3. To serve, top with remaining dessert topping. If desired, garnish with additional strawberries.

TROUBLE IN PARADISE???

THAT'S **NOT** WHAT I NEEDED TO HEAR RIGHT NOW, BRAD. BUT I CAN SUBSTITUTE MILK FOR THE CRÈME DE CACAO.

NUTRITION FACTS PER SERVING: 246 calories, 9 g total fat (4 g saturated fat), 7 mg cholesterol, 143 mg sodium, 38 g carbohydrate, 1 g fiber, 2 g protein. Daily Values: 3% vit. A, 47% vit. C, 4% calcium, 7% iron.

QUICK & CREAMY RICE PUDDING

FOR MYSTERIOUS REASONS, RICE PUDDING GETS COOKS YAMMERING ON ABOUT TECHNIQUE. THIS ONE WILL TURN THE TALK TOWARD FLAVOR!

INGREDIENTS

Makes 4 servings

Start to finish: 25 min.

- 1 4-serving-size package instant vanilla pudding mix
- 1¼ cups milk
- 1 cup quick-cooking white rice
- ¼ cup dried tart cherries or blueberries, or snipped dried apricots
- ¼ teaspoon ground cardamom or cinnamon

✓ "Pantry Only... no shopping required!"

DIRECTIONS

1. Prepare pudding mix according to package directions; set aside.

2. Meanwhile, heat milk over medium heat just to boiling. Stir in rice and dried fruit. Remove from heat; cover and let stand 5 minutes. Stir in prepared vanilla pudding and cardamom. Serve warm or cover surface with plastic wrap and chill.

NUTRITION FACTS PER SERVING: 234 calories, 2 g total fat (1 g saturated fat), 6 mg cholesterol, 178 mg sodium, 51 g carbohydrate, 0 g fiber, 5 g protein. Daily Values: 9% vit. A, 1% vit. C, 8% calcium, 7% iron.

EASY APPLE & OATMEAL CRISP

SCIENTISTS WON'T CONFIRM WHY, BUT WHEN FALL COMES, HUMANS GET AN INNATE URGE TO BAKE HOMEY DESSERTS. WHEN THAT HAPPENS, TRY THIS.

INGREDIENTS

Makes 6 to 8 servings
Prep: 10 min. Bake: 25 min.

- 1   cup all-purpose flour
- ¾ cup packed brown sugar
- ¼ teaspoon salt
- ½ cup butter or margarine
- 1   cup rolled oats
- 1   21-ounce can apple pie filling

✓ "Pantry Only... no shopping required!"

DIRECTIONS

1. In a large mixing bowl stir together flour, brown sugar, and salt. Cut in butter until mixture resembles coarse crumbs; stir in oats. Press about 2 cups of the mixture into a greased 2-quart square baking dish. Top evenly with pie filling. Sprinkle remaining crumb mixture on top. Bake in a 375° oven for 25 minutes. Serve warm.

NOTE: Try topping warm apple crisp with a scoop of ice cream—Mmmm!

IT WAS JUST A SUGGESTION...

HOW ABOUT A SCOOP OF RICH, DELECTABLE, VANILLA ICE CREAM MELTING OVER THIS WARM APPLE CRISP ...

OH, HONEY, THAT SOUNDS DIVINE!

NUTRITION FACTS PER SERVING: 438 calories, 16 g total fat (10 g saturated fat), 41 mg cholesterol, 294 mg sodium, 71 g carbohydrate, 2 g fiber, 4 g protein. Daily Values: 24% vit. A, 17% vit. C, 3% calcium, 15% iron.

FAMILY STYLE BANANAS FOSTER

FANCY RESTAURANTS USED TO FLAMBÉ THIS DESSERT TABLESIDE, A PRACTICE THAT'S A BIT TRICKY. NO SUCH PYROTECHNICS NEEDED HERE!

INGREDIENTS

Makes 4 servings
Start to finish: 10 min.

- 2 tablespoons butter or margarine
- ¼ cup packed brown sugar
- 4 ripe bananas, halved lengthwise and then crosswise
- ½ teaspoon cinnamon
- 2 tablespoons orange liqueur or orange juice
- 2 cups vanilla ice cream

✓ *Grocery List*
  BANANAS

DIRECTIONS

1. In a 10-inch skillet melt butter; stir in brown sugar until melted. Add bananas; cook and stir gently over medium heat about 2 minutes or until heated through. Sprinkle with cinnamon. Stir in orange liqueur. Spoon warm banana mixture over ice cream. Serve immediately.

FOSTERING CUSTOMER TIES

BANANAS FOSTER ORIGINATES FROM BRENNAN'S, A FAMOUS NEW ORLEANS RESTAURANT. IN THE 1950S A CUSTOMER NAMED RICHARD FOSTER FREQUENTED THE RESTAURANT, AND HE MUST HAVE GONE BANANAS OVER THIS DESSERT (OR PERHAPS THE RESTAURANT WENT BANANAS OVER ALL HIS PATRONAGE), FOR BRENNAN'S ALLEGEDLY NAMED THE DESSERT AFTER FOSTER.

NUTRITION FACTS PER SERVING: 349 calories, 14 g total fat (8 g saturated fat), 44 mg cholesterol, 115 mg sodium, 55 g carbohydrate, 2 g fiber, 4 g protein. Daily Values: 13% vit. A, 17% vit. C, 8% calcium, 5% iron.

DESSERT BERRY SOUP WITH SORBET

FINALLY—FOOD FOR YOUR EVERY MOOD! THE VARIATIONS ON THIS THEME RANGE FROM FROM FRUITY AND LIGHT TO CHOCOLATEY RICH.

INGREDIENTS

Makes 4 servings

Start to finish: 20 min.

- 2 cups frozen unsweetened blueberries
- 1 10-ounce package frozen sliced strawberries in syrup
- ½ teaspoon finely shredded orange peel (optional)
- ¾ cup orange juice
- 2 cups orange or other fruit sorbet or sherbet
- 4 sprigs fresh mint (optional)

✓ *Grocery List*

ORANGE
ORANGE SORBET OR SHERBET
FRESH MINT

DIRECTIONS

1. In a medium saucepan combine the frozen blueberries with their syrup, *half* of the strawberries, the orange peel (if using), and orange juice. Cook over medium heat, stirring occasionally, for 4 to 5 minutes or just until the berries are thawed. Remove from heat. Stir in the remaining frozen blueberries; let stand about 5 minutes to thaw the berries and cool the mixture slightly.

2. When the berries are completely thawed, ladle the soup into 4 shallow dessert bowls. Top each with a scoop of sorbet. If desired, garnish with mint.

BERRY-CHOCOLATE SOUP: Prepare as above, except substitute chocolate ice cream or sorbet for fruit sorbet. Garnish with white chocolate shavings.

WARM FRUIT SOUP WITH VANILLA ICE CREAM: Prepare as above, except heat with all of the blueberries; do not cool. Substitute vanilla ice cream for the fruit sorbet. Drizzle with chocolate-flavored syrup.

DESSERT PEACH AND BERRY SOUP: Prepare as above, except substitute one 10-ounce package frozen red raspberries in syrup for the frozen strawberries. Substitute vanilla ice cream for the fruit sorbet. Serve with 2 cups thawed, frozen unsweetened peach slices.

NUTRITION FACTS PER SERVING: 262 calories, 2 g total fat (1 g saturated fat), 5 mg cholesterol, 37 mg sodium, 63 g carbohydrate, 8 g fiber, 2 g protein. Daily Values: 3% vit. A, 110% vit. C, 5% calcium, 4% iron.

STRAWBERRY RICOTTA ROLLS

TORTILLAS FOR DESSERT? SURE! HERE, THEY WORK LIKE CREPES, BUT YOU DON'T HAVE TO HASSLE WITH BATTER AND A FANCY PAN.

INGREDIENTS

Makes 4 servings
Prep: 1 min. **Cook:** 4 min.

- 1 cup whole milk ricotta cheese
- 1 10-ounce package frozen sliced strawberries in syrup
- 2 tablespoons sugar
- 1 teaspoon vanilla
- ¼ teaspoon ground cinnamon (optional)
- 4 7-inch flour tortillas
- 2 teaspoons butter or margarine
  Sifted powdered sugar (optional)

✓ *Grocery List*
  RICOTTA CHEESE

DIRECTIONS

1. Allow ricotta cheese to stand at room temperature for 30 minutes. Meanwhile, for sauce, place frozen berries with their syrup in a medium saucepan; heat over medium-low until warm; set sauce aside.
2. For filling, in a small bowl combine ricotta cheese, sugar, vanilla, and, if desired, cinnamon. Place a quarter of the filling in the center of each tortilla. Fold opposite sides in. Carefully roll up from bottoms, tucking in the ends.
3. Heat the butter in a large nonstick skillet over medium heat; carefully add the tortilla rolls. Cook for 4 to 5 minutes or until well browned and crisp, turning halfway through.
4. Top each tortilla roll with some of the sauce. If desired, sprinkle with powdered sugar. Serve immediately.

USING TORTILLAS – IN NOTHING FLAT!

TORTILLAS ARE A QUICK AND EASY BREAD SOURCE. YOU CAN KEEP THEM IN THE FREEZER AND DEFROST THEM QUICKLY IN THE REFRIGERATOR, MICROWAVE, OR AT ROOM TEMPERATURE. YOU CAN ALSO QUICKLY DEFROST TORTILLAS BY HEATING THEM IN A SKILLET, TURNING A COUPLE OF TIMES WITH TONGS. FOR THIS RECIPE, HEATING THE TORTILLAS FOR JUST A COUPLE OF SECONDS BEFOREHAND WILL MAKE ROLLING THEM EASIER.

NUTRITION FACTS PER SERVING: 308 calories, 12 g total fat (7 g saturated fat), 36 mg cholesterol, 193 mg sodium, 42 g carbohydrate, 6 g fiber, 9 g protein. Daily Values: 10% vit. A, 49% vit. C, 13% calcium, 10% iron.

RASPBERRY & CHOCOLATE TULIPS

PHYLLO DOUGH SHELLS OFFER ALL THE FLAKINESS OF TRADITIONAL PHYLLO SHEETS, BUT THEY'RE EASIER TO USE. (KEEP THAT TO YOURSELF!)

INGREDIENTS

Makes 15 tulips

Start to finish: 15 min.

- ½ cup frozen raspberries
- 2 tablespoons sugar
- 1 2.1-ounce package (15) miniature phyllo dough shells
- 4 teaspoons chocolate-flavored syrup
- 15 little squirts from a 7-ounce can pressurized whipped dessert topping
- 1½ tablespoons sliced almonds (optional)

✓ *Grocery List*
   WHIPPED DESSERT TOPPING

DIRECTIONS

1. Combine raspberries and sugar in a small saucepan. Cook over medium heat, stirring frequently, for 3 to 5 minutes or just until the sugar is melted and raspberries are completely thawed. Remove from heat; cool until slightly warm or room temperature.

2. To serve, place the phyllo dough shells on a platter. Spoon about ½ teaspoon raspberry mixture into the bottom of each shell, followed by about ¼ teaspoon chocolate-flavored syrup and a squirt of whipped dessert topping. If desired, sprinkle with almonds. Serve immediately.

ICE CREAM TULIPS: Prepare as above, except substitute softened ice cream for the raspberry mixture.

NUTRITION FACTS PER TULIP: 46 calories, 2 g total fat (0 g saturated fat), 0 mg cholesterol, 11 mg sodium, 6 g carbohydrate, 0 g fiber, 0 g protein. Daily Values: 0% vit. A, 1% vit. C, 0% calcium, 1% iron.

DESSERT WAFFLES WITH RASPBERRY COULIS

THINK OUTSIDE THE BOX! A BREAKFAST FAVORITE BECOMES DESSERT WHEN YOU ADD A RASPBERRY SAUCE (CALLED "COULIS") AND ICE CREAM.

INGREDIENTS

Makes 6 servings
Start to finish: 10 min.

- 1 10-ounce package frozen raspberries in syrup, thawed
- ¼ cup sifted powdered sugar
- 2 tablespoons crème de cassis (optional)
- 6 frozen waffles, toasted
- 3 cups vanilla ice cream
  Sifted powdered sugar (optional)

✓ Grocery List
  FROZEN WAFFLES (IF THIS BECOMES A FAVORITE DESSERT, ADD FROZEN WAFFLES TO YOUR PANTRY LIST!)
  VANILLA ICE CREAM

DIRECTIONS

1. For coulis, press raspberries and syrup through a fine-mesh sieve; discard seeds. In a small bowl combine sieved berries, the ¼ cup powdered sugar, and créme de cassis, if desired.

2. To serve, cut each waffle diagonally in half. Place 2 waffle halves on each of 6 dessert plates; top with ice cream. Drizzle with coulis. If desired, dust with additional powdered sugar.

NUTRITION FACTS PER SERVING: 300 calories, 11 g total fat (4 g saturated fat), 29 mg cholesterol, 310 mg sodium, 48 g carbohydrate, 3 g fiber, 5 g protein. Daily Values: 17% vit. A, 13% vit. C, 10% calcium, 14% iron.

BLACK FOREST SHORTCAKES

CALL IT A SHORTCAKE, BABYCAKE, OR TORTE—JUST DON'T TELL THEM IT STARTS WITH A PURCHASED MUFFIN—THEY'LL FALL FOR IT EVERY TIME!

INGREDIENTS

Makes 4 servings
Prep: 1 min. **Cook:** 15 min.

- ½ cup semisweet chocolate pieces
- 2 tablespoons butter or margarine
- ¼ cup black cherry spreadable fruit
- 1 to 2 tablespoons sugar
- ½ of a 5-ounce can (⅓ cup) evaporated milk
- 4 chocolate muffins
- ½ cup whipping cream, whipped
- 4 maraschino cherries (optional)

✓ *Grocery List*
   BLACK CHERRY SPREADABLE FRUIT
   CHOCOLATE MUFFINS OR
      CUPCAKES
   WHIPPING CREAM

DIRECTIONS

1. For sauce, in a small heavy saucepan melt the chocolate pieces and butter; add spreadable fruit and sugar. Gradually stir in evaporated milk. Bring mixture to boiling. Reduce heat and simmer, uncovered, for 5 minutes, stirring frequently. Cool slightly.

2. Split muffins into 2 layers. Spoon *half* of the whipped cream and *half* of the sauce over the first layer. Top with second layer, remaining whipped cream, and sauce. If desired, top each with a maraschino cherry. Serve immediately.

WASTE??? NOT!!!

I'M NOT SURE HOW TO BREAK THIS TO YOU, BUT WE'VE GOT SOME EXTRA SAUCE LEFT.

BUT JUST IMAGINE HOW GREAT IT WILL TASTE ON ICE CREAM! LET'S STORE IT TIGHTLY SEALED IN THE REFRIGERATOR FOR A COUPLE OF DAYS.

NUTRITION FACTS PER SERVING: 554 calories, 28 g total fat (12 g saturated fat), 89 mg cholesterol, 332 mg sodium, 76 g carbohydrate, 1 g fiber, 5 g protein. Daily Values: 20% vit. A, 0% vit. C, 10% calcium, 8% iron.

FAST & FRUITY BANANA SPLIT TARTS

NEXT TIME SOMEONE WEASELS YOU INTO MAKING DESSERT, DON'T GET MAD. GET SOME PHYLLO SHELLS AND MAKE THIS NO-BAKE, MAKE-AHEAD TREAT.

INGREDIENTS

Makes 15 tarts

Start to finish: 10 min.

- 1 8-ounce tub cream cheese with pineapple
- ¼ cup strawberry preserves
- 1 2.1-ounce package (15) miniature phyllo dough shells
- 1 banana, thinly sliced
- ⅓ cup chocolate ice cream topping

✓ *Grocery List*
**CREAM CHEESE WITH PINEAPPLE
BANANA**

DIRECTIONS

1. For filling, in a small mixing bowl, beat the cream cheese and preserves until light and fluffy. Spoon filling into each shell. If desired, cover and refrigerate for up to 4 hours. To serve, divide banana slices among shells. Drizzle with ice cream topping. Serve immediately.

NUTRITION FACTS PER TART: 115 calories, 6 g total fat (3 g saturated fat), 13 mg cholesterol, 63 mg sodium, 14 g carbohydrate, 0 g fiber, 1 g protein. Daily Values: 2% vit. A, 1% vit. C, 1% calcium, 2% iron.

RASPBERRIES ON A CITRUS CLOUD

THE LOW-FAT CROWD OUGHT TO LOVE THIS ONE-FAT-GRAM WONDER—AND EVEN IF YOU COULDN'T CARE LESS ABOUT SUCH THINGS, IT'S LUSCIOUS!

INGREDIENTS

Makes 4 servings

Start to finish: 15 min.

- 2 cups fresh red raspberries
- 4 teaspoons raspberry liqueur (optional)
- 1 8-ounce carton lemon-flavored yogurt
- ¼ of an 8-ounce container frozen fat-free whipped dessert topping, thawed
- 3 tablespoons sugar

✓ *Grocery List*

LEMON YOGURT
WHIPPED DESSERT TOPPING
FRESH RASPBERRIES

DIRECTIONS

1. Reserve ¼ *cup* of the raspberries. In a medium bowl gently toss remaining raspberries with liqueur, if desired.

2. In a small bowl stir together yogurt and dessert topping. Spoon berry-liqueur mixture into four dessert dishes. Dollop yogurt mixture onto berries. Serve immediately or cover and chill up to 4 hours.

3. Just before serving, place sugar in a heavy saucepan. Heat over medium-high heat until sugar begins to melt, shaking pan occasionally to heat sugar evenly. *Do not stir.* Once the sugar starts to melt, reduce heat to low and cook about 5 minutes more or until all of the sugar is melted and golden, stirring as needed with a wooden spoon. Remove pan from heat. Let stand for 1 minute. Dip a fork into caramelized sugar and let syrup run off tines of fork for several seconds before gently shaking the fork over the yogurt mixture, allowing thin strands of caramelized sugar to drizzle over berries. (If sugar starts to harden in the pan, return to heat, stirring until melted.) Top with reserved raspberries. Serve immediately.

NUTRITION FACTS PER SERVING: 148 calories, 1 g total fat (0 g saturated fat), 2 mg cholesterol, 41 mg sodium, 32 g carbohydrate, 3 g fiber, 3 g protein. Daily Values: 1% vit. A, 26% vit. C, 8% calcium, 2% iron.

103

BLUEBERRY RHUBARB CRISP

RHUBARB IS WONDERFULLY TART, BUT CAN SOMETIMES BENEFIT FROM A CIVILIZING INFLUENCE, SUCH AS THE BLUEBERRIES IN THIS HOMEY CRISP.

INGREDIENTS

Makes 6 servings
Prep: 10 min. **Bake:** 30 min.

- 3 cups fresh or frozen unsweetened blueberries
- 2 cups fresh or frozen unsweetened sliced rhubarb
- ½ cup regular rolled oats
- ½ cup all-purpose flour
- ½ cup packed brown sugar
- ½ teaspoon ground cinnamon
- ¼ cup butter

✓ *Grocery List*
   BLUEBERRIES
   RHUBARB

DIRECTIONS

1. For filling, thaw fruit if frozen. *Do not drain.* Place fruit in a 2-quart square baking dish.

2. For topping, in a medium bowl combine the oats, flour, brown sugar, and cinnamon. Cut in butter until mixture resembles coarse crumbs. Sprinkle topping over filling.

3. Bake in a 350° oven for 30 to 35 minutes (40 minutes for frozen fruit) or until fruit is tender and topping is golden. Serve warm.

JUST SAY NO!

WHEN BUYING RHUBARB, LOOK FOR STALKS THAT ARE TENDER AND FIRM; IF THE RHUBARB IS WILTED-LOOKING OR HAS THICK STALKS, DON'T BUY IT. YOU CAN SUBSTITUTE FROZEN UNSWEETENED SLICED RHUBARB IN THIS RECIPE.

NUTRITION FACTS PER SERVING: 233 calories, 8 g total fat (5 g saturated fat), 20 mg cholesterol, 88 mg sodium, 38 g carbohydrate, 3 g fiber, 3 g protein. Daily Values: 8% vit. A, 21 % vit. C, 5% calcium, 9% iron.

CHERRY & CHOCOLATE HEARTS

A SUPER-FANCY DESSERT WITH JUST FOUR INGREDIENTS? PUFF PASTRY MAKES IT SO! IF THE FUDGE IS TOO THICK TO DRIZZLE, GENTLY WARM IT.

INGREDIENTS

Makes 8 servings

Prep: 10 min. **Bake:** 15 min.

- ½ of a 17¼-ounce package (1 sheet) frozen puff pastry, thawed
- ¾ cup cherry pie filling
- 8 teaspoons fudge ice cream topping, warmed
- 2 tablespoons chopped nuts

✓ "Pantry Only... no shopping required!"

DIRECTIONS

1. On a lightly floured surface, unfold thawed puff pastry. Using a 3½- to 4-inch heart-shaped cookie cutter, cut pastry into 8 pastry hearts, discarding scraps or reserving for another use. Place pastry hearts on an ungreased cookie sheet. Bake in a 375° oven for 15 to 18 minutes or until puffed and golden. Cool on wire racks.

2. To serve, split hearts horizontally. Fill each heart with some of the pie filling. Place hearts on dessert plates. Drizzle with ice cream topping; sprinkle with nuts. Serve immediately.

NOTE: Heat fudge topping if too thick to drizzle.

THE WAY TO EVERYONE'S HEART

TASTY, GORGEOUS TO LOOK AT, ADAPTABLE, FAST, AND EASY TO USE . . . I LOVE USING FROZEN PUFF PASTRY FOR DESSERTS! PLUS, I CAN ADAPT THIS RECIPE TO ANY OCCASION BY REPLACING THE HEART-SHAPED COOKIE CUTTER WITH ANY SHAPE I LIKE.

NUTRITION FACTS PER SERVING: 191 calories, 12 g total fat (1 g saturated fat), 0 mg cholesterol, 121 mg sodium, 21 g carbohydrate, 0 g fiber, 2 g protein. Daily Values: 0% vit. A, 0 % vit. C, 1% calcium, 1% iron.

105

FRUIT-FILLED NAPOLEONS

VITE! VITE! THAT'S WHAT NAPOLEON MIGHT SAY IF HE WERE WAITING FOR THESE—YOU'LL NEED TO SERVE THEM **QUICKLY**, OR THEY'LL GET SOGGY.

INGREDIENTS

Makes 8 servings
Prep: 20 min. **Bake:** 20 min.

- ½ of a 17¼-ounce package (1 sheet) puff pastry, thawed
- 2 cups pudding, fruit-flavored yogurt, sweetened whipped cream, or softened ice cream
- 1 cup peeled and sliced kiwi fruit, halved seedless red grapes, berries, and/or halved orange slices

   Sifted powdered sugar (optional)

✓ Grocery List

PUDDING, YOGURT, WHIPPED CREAM, OR ICE CREAM
KIWI FRUIT; GRAPES; BERRIES AND/OR ORANGES

DIRECTIONS

1. On a lightly floured surface, unfold thawed pastry. Using a small sharp knife, cut pastry into 8 rectangles (each the same size). Place pastry rectangles on an ungreased cookie sheet. Bake in a 375° oven about 20 minutes or until puffed and golden. Cool on wire racks.

2. Just before serving, split each pastry rectangle in half horizontally. Spoon pudding into pastry bottoms. Top with fruit and pastry tops. If desired, sprinkle tops with powdered sugar. Serve immediately.

NAPOLEON WHO?

THIS CLASSIC IS A SPECIALTY OF—WHERE ELSE—FRANCE. IT GENERALLY FEATURES PUFF PASTRY LAYERED WITH RICH PASTRY CREAM (WE USE PUDDING—IT'S EASIER TO MAKE). THE FRUIT IS A BIT OF AN ABERRATION FROM THE ORIGINAL, BUT IT ADDS COLOR AND TEXTURE.

YES, THE DESSERT WAS NAMED FOR THE LITTLE GENERAL. NO, JOSEPHINE PROBABLY DIDN'T INVENT IT.

NUTRITION FACTS PER SERVING: 266 calories, 13 g total fat (0 g saturated fat), 1 mg cholesterol, 184 mg sodium, 35 g carbohydrate, 1 g fiber, 3 g protein. Daily Value: 4% vit. A, 67% vit. C, 8% calcium, 2% iron.

MOCHA PEARS

HOW ABOUT ANOTHER ONE SNAGGED FROM THE FRENCH? IT'S MODELED AFTER "POIRE BELLE HÉLÈNE," A SORT OF HOT-FUDGE PEAR SUNDAE.

INGREDIENTS

Makes 6 servings

Prep: 10 min. **Cook:** 15 min. **Chill:** 4 hrs.

- 2 **16-ounce cans or one 29-ounce can (12) pear halves in heavy syrup**
- 2 **teaspoons instant coffee crystals**
- 1 **teaspoon vanilla**
- ¾ **cup vanilla yogurt**

  Chocolate curls or miniature semisweet chocolate pieces

✓ *Grocery List*
  VANILLA YOGURT

DIRECTIONS

1. Drain pears, reserving syrup. Place pears in a bowl; set aside.

2. In a saucepan combine the reserved pear syrup and coffee crystals. Bring to boiling. Reduce heat and simmer, uncovered, about 15 minutes or until slightly thickened and reduced to ½ cup. Stir in the vanilla. Pour syrup-and-coffee mixture over pears. Cover and refrigerate for several hours, turning pears once.

3. To serve, using a slotted spoon, place 2 pear halves into each of 6 dessert dishes. Top each serving with some of the reduced syrup and 2 tablespoons yogurt. Garnish each serving with chocolate curls.

NUTRITION FACTS PER SERVING: 149 calories, 1 g total fat, (0 g saturated fat), 2 mg cholesterol, 30 mg sodium, 33 g carbohydrate, 1 g fiber, 1 g protein. Daily Values: 0% vit. A, 5 % vit. C, 3% calcium, 0% iron.

107

MANGO PARFAITS

EVERYBODY DOESN'T LIKE SOMETHING—BUT WHO WOULDN'T LIKE MAKING A RICH, FRUITY DESSERT THAT STARTS WITH FROZEN POUND CAKE?

INGREDIENTS

Makes 4 servings

Start to finish: 20 min.

- ½ of a 10¾-ounce frozen loaf pound cake or frozen reduced-calorie loaf pound cake, thawed and cut into ½-inch cubes
- ¼ cup amaretto or other almond-flavored liqueur, or ¼ cup orange juice plus ¼ teaspoon almond extract
- 1 8-ounce carton fat-free or light dairy sour cream
- 2 tablespoons powdered sugar
- 2 ripe mangoes, peeled, seeded, and cut into ½-inch pieces
  Fresh fruit (such as sliced kiwi fruit, raspberries, or strawberries) (optional)

✓ *Grocery List*
POUND CAKE (FROZEN POUND CAKE CAN BE KEPT ON HAND)
SOUR CREAM
MANGOS
FRESH FRUIT

DIRECTIONS

1. Toss cake cubes with *half* of the amaretto. Combine remaining amaretto, sour cream, and powdered sugar.

2. To serve, place a few cake cubes into the bottom of a parfait glass followed by about *1 tablespoon* of the sour cream mixture. Add a layer of mangoes. Repeat until glass is full. Repeat with three more glasses. Serve immediately or cover and chill up to 1 hour. If desired, garnish with fruit.

NUTRITION FACTS PER SERVING: 320 calories, 8 g total fat (4 g saturated fat), 0 mg cholesterol, 189 mg sodium, 53 g carbohydrate, 2 g fiber, 6 g protein. Daily Values: 53% vit. A, 47% vit. C, 9% calcium, 4% iron.

CANDY-BAR DESSERT PIZZA

BROWNIES, CANDY BARS, ICE CREAM, BUTTERSCOTCH TOPPING, NUTS—ALL AT ONCE? WHY NOT? YOU'RE THE ADULT—YOU MAKE THE RULES!

INGREDIENTS

Makes 12 servings
Prep: 15 min. **Bake:** 18 min.
Freeze: 1 hr.

- 1   19½ to 21½-ounce package fudge brownie mix
- ½   cup water
- ¼   cup cooking oil
- 1   egg
- 1   quart chocolate ice cream
- ½   cup butterscotch, caramel, fudge, or marshmallow ice cream topping, warmed
- 2   cups cut-up candy bars (chocolate-coated caramel-topped nougat bars, chocolate-covered English toffee, chocolate-covered peanut butter cups, and/or white chocolate candy bars)
- ¼   cup chopped nuts (optional)
  Sliced fresh strawberries (optional)

✓ *Grocery List*
   CHOCOLATE ICE CREAM
   WHIPPING CREAM
   CANDY BARS
   STRAWBERRIES

DIRECTIONS

1. In a large mixing bowl combine brownie mix, water, oil, and egg; stir until combined. Spread dough evenly into a greased 12-inch pizza pan with ½-inch sides. Bake in a 375° oven for 18 to 20 minutes. Cool completely.

2. Cut brownie into 12 wedges; do not remove from pan. Place small scoops of chocolate ice cream on each wedge. Cover tightly and freeze until firm.

3. To serve, pour warm ice cream topping over ice cream. Sprinkle with cut-up candy bars. If desired, sprinkle with chopped nuts and garnish with fresh strawberries. Serve immediately.

INDEX

By making a few conversions, cooks in Australia, Canada, and the United Kingdom can use the recipes in this book with confidence. The charts on this page provide a guide for converting measurements from the U.S. customary system, which is used throughout this book, to the imperial and metric systems. There also is a conversion table for oven temperatures to accommodate the differences in oven calibrations.

PRODUCT DIFFERENCES: Most of the ingredients called for in the recipes in this book are available in English-speaking countries. However, some are known by different names. Here are some common U.S. American ingredients and their possible counterparts:

• Sugar is granulated or castor sugar.
• Powdered sugar is icing sugar.
• All-purpose flour is plain household flour or white flour. When self-rising flour is used in place of all-purpose flour in a recipe that calls for leavening, omit the leavening agent (baking soda or baking powder) and salt.
• Light-colored corn syrup is golden syrup.
• Cornstarch is cornflour.
• Baking soda is bicarbonate of soda.
• Vanilla is vanilla essence.
• Green, red, or yellow sweet peppers are capsicums.
• Golden raisins are sultanas.

VOLUME AND WEIGHT: U.S. Americans traditionally use cup measures for liquid and solid ingredients. The chart, above right, shows the approximate imperial and metric equivalents. If you are accustomed to weighing solid ingredients, the following approximate equivalents will help.
• 1 cup butter, castor sugar, or rice = 8 ounces = about 230 grams
• 1 cup flour = 4 ounces = about 115 grams
• 1 cup icing sugar = 5 ounces = about 140 grams

Spoon measures are used for smaller amounts of ingredients. Although the size of the tablespoon varies slightly in different countries, for practical purposes and for recipes in this book, a straight substitution is all that's necessary. Measurements made using cups or spoons always should be level unless stated otherwise.

EQUIVALENTS: U.S. = AUSTRALIA/U.K.

⅓ teaspoon = 1 ml
¼ teaspoon = 1.25 ml
½ teaspoon = 2.5 ml
1 teaspoon = 5 ml
1 tablespoon = 15 ml
1 fluid ounce = 30 ml
¼ cup = 60 ml
⅓ cup = 80 ml
½ cup = 120 ml
⅔ cup = 160 ml
¾ cup = 180 ml
1 cup = 240 ml
2 cups = 475 ml
1 quart = 1 liter
½ inch = 1.25 cm
1 inch = 2.5 cm

BAKING PAN SIZES

American	Metric
8×1½-inch round baking pan	20×4-cm cake tin
9×1½-inch round baking pan	23×4-cm cake tin
11×7×1½-inch baking pan	28×18×4-cm baking tin
13×9×2-inch baking pan	32×23×5-cm baking tin
2-quart rectangular baking dish	28×18×4-cm baking tin
15×10×1-inch baking pan	38×25.5×2.5-cm baking tin (Swiss roll tin)
9-inch pie plate	22×4- or 23×4-cm pie plate
7- or 8-inch springform pan	18- or 20-cm springform or loose-bottom cake tin
9×5×3-inch loaf pan	23×13×8-cm or 2-pound narrow loaf tin or pâté tin
1½-quart casserole	1.5-liter casserole
2-quart casserole	2-liter casserole

OVEN TEMPERATURE EQUIVALENTS

Fahrenheit Setting	Celsius Setting*	Gas Setting
300°F	150°C	Gas mark 2 (very low)
325°F	170°C	Gas mark 3 (low)
350°F	180°C	Gas mark 4 (moderate)
375°F	190°C	Gas mark 5 (moderately hot)
400°F	200°C	Gas mark 6 (hot)
425°F	220°C	Gas mark 7 (hot)
450°F	230°C	Gas mark 8 (very hot)
475°F	240°C	Gas mark 9 (very hot)
Broil		Grill

*Electric and gas ovens may be calibrated using Celsius. However, for an electric oven, increase the Celsius setting 10 to 20 degrees when cooking above 160°C. For convection or forced-air ovens (gas or electric), lower the temperature setting 10°C when cooking at all heat levels.